Knit|So Fine

DESIGNS WITH SKINNY YARN

Lisa R. MYERS,
Laura GRUTZECK,
and Carol SULCOSKI

INTERWEAVE PRESS
interweavebooks.com

Model photography by Joe Coca
Tabletop photography by Ann Swanson
Illustrations by Gayle Ford
Technical editing by Donna Druchunas
Text © 2008 Lisa R. Myers, Laura Grutzeck,
  and Carol Sulcoski
Photography © 2008 Interweave Press LLC
Illustrations © 2008 Interweave Press LLC

Interweave Press LLC
201 East Fourth Street
Loveland, CO 80537-5655 USA
interweavebooks.com

Printed in China by Asia Pacific Offset

Library of Congress
Cataloging-in-Publication Data

Myers, Lisa R.
  Knit so fine : designs with skinny yarn / Lisa R. Myers,
Laura Grutzeck, and Carol Sulcoski, authors.
     p. cm.
  Includes index.
  ISBN 978-1-59668-052-4 (pbk.)
  1. Knitting--Patterns. 2. Yarn. I. Grutzeck, Laura,
1968- II. Sulcoski, Carol, 1965- III. Title.
  TT820.M9677 2008
  746.43'2--dc22

                              2007036777

10 9 8 7 6 5 4 3 2 1

To the knitters out there who are always willing to take the next step. —L.R.M.

To my grandmother and my Tante Frieda; I am proud to knit like you. —L.G.

To my beloved children, James, Nick, and Grace, in appreciation for all the times they heard "Just let Mommy finish one more row." —C.S.

Acknowledgments

To accomplish a book containing over twenty items knitted at small gauges in less than a year was no small feat, and we are deeply grateful to all those who helped make it possible, including: our editors, Ann Budd and Tricia Waddell, for their patience and good humor; our eagle-eyed technical editor, Donna Druchunas; Rebecca Campbell, for her enthusiasm in managing the book; Joe Coca for the beautiful photography. We'd also like to thank the customers and staff members of Rosie's Yarn Cellar, current and past, who showed us their encouragement and support, and our test knitters, who were accommodating and patient above and beyond the call of duty: Shea Cronley, Emily Gavin, Wendy Goldstein, Suzanne Litke, Mindy Soucek, Dorlynn Starn, Karen R. Walter, Judy Wise.

LISA | I would like to thank Judith Shangold, for bearing with one more disruption, and my family, for recognizing that one person's hobby is another person's job.

LAURA | In addition, I would like to thank my family for their encouragement, my husband, Chris, for always believing in me, and my friend Anne for always listening.

CAROL | I would like to thank my parents for their unstinting confidence that I could do whatever I set my mind to do (even if it meant abandoning that expensive legal education); Molly and Pat for their years of devoted friendship; Mindy, for going above and beyond the call of duty; the Wolvies (including Kathy), who always make me laugh; the many wonderful people whom I've met through the real world and online knitting community (you know who you are); Dr. S and his staff for their compassion in helping me get my life back; and for my family, Tom, James, Nick, Grace, and Charcoal.

The Projects

SIMPLICITY 32

Ruffle Scarf 34
Drapey Silk Top 36
Cowlneck Pullover 40
Cabled Vest 44
Kimono Top 48

SPEED 52

Ribby Vest 54
Anemone Beret 58
Eyelet Halter 60
Mohair T-Neck 64
Dolman Top 68

Contents

INTRODUCTION 6

THE SKINNY ON FINE YARNS 9

TOOLS, TIPS, AND TECHNIQUES 21

GLOSSARY 135

SOURCES FOR SUPPLIES 141

BIBLIOGRAPHY 142

INDEX 143

STYLE 72
    Skater Sweater 74
    Lace-Trimmed Raglan 78
    Wrap Dress 82
    Bamboo Skirt 90
    Asymmetric Cardigan 94

SHINE 98
    Bohus-Inspired Pullover 100
    Traveling Stitch Legwarmers 106
    Lattice Lace Pullover 112
    Zip-Front Hoodie 118
    Lace Stole 124
    Fingerless Elbow Gloves 130

Introduction

Skinny yarns get a really bad rap. Knitters have somehow gotten the idea that they're slow, fussy, or old-fashioned. We're here to prove otherwise. Thin yarns offer a world of possibilities; in fact, they can do anything a thick yarn can do and more—and often, they do it better. Projects knitted with thin yarns can be quick, easy, daring, or bold—though it's certainly true that they can be elaborate, refined, or demure. The projects in this book are designed to disprove the myths you may have heard about fine yarns and to show you things you haven't imagined.

We'll start our journey by educating you about fine yarns: what they are, the many advantages of knitting with fine yarns, and tips and techniques to make the process more enjoyable. Then we'll show you some patterns: patterns that are contemporary and stylish and demonstrate some of the wonderful uses of fine yarns. To make it even easier to dive in, we've grouped the patterns into four sections, depending on the kind of project you're looking for:

SIMPLICITY includes patterns that are particularly accessible to knitters who don't have a lot of experience with fine yarns; it's the perfect way to get accustomed to working with thin needles and skinny yarns.

SPEED debunks the myth that projects in fine yarns take forever to finish. We'll give you some small projects that you can finish quickly for a satisfying sense of accomplishment. We'll also show you how to use fine yarns in different ways—double-stranding or knitting at looser gauges—for times when speed is important.

STYLE showcases some of the contemporary and fashionable ways to use fine yarns—no potato-sack garments here.

SHINE contains boundary-busting possibilities and more advanced projects to get your creative juices flowing, including lace, traveling stitches, and cables.

Throughout the book, we've included sidebars to help you through unfamiliar techniques and design challenges and to point you toward areas you may want to explore in greater depth on your own.

So cast aside those misconceptions, abandon those preconceived notions, and allow us to bust some myths. It's time to get the skinny on fine yarns.

What is a "Fine" Yarn?

For purposes of this book, a "fine" yarn is any yarn that knits at a gauge finer than worsted weight (i.e., yarns that knit up at 5½, 6, 7, or more stitches per inch, or yarns that are classified by the Craft Yarn Council in categories 3, 2, 1, or 0). Admittedly, this is an arbitrary way to look at it, but our experience is that most knitters draw a conceptual line between worsted-weight yarns (i.e., yarns that knit up at 4½ to 5 stitches to the inch) and thinner yarns. We've tried to use a variety of yarn weights within the category of "fine" yarns so you'll have ample opportunity to experiment with a variety of skinny yarns.

Standard Yarn, Needle Sizes, and Gauges

Gauge	Yarn Size	Needle Size	(stitches/4")
#0	Lace (lace)	U.S. 000–1 1.5–2.25 mm	33–40
#1	Super Fine (fingering)	U.S. 1–3 2.25–3.25 mm	27–32
#2	Fine (sport)	U.S. 3–5 3.25–3.75 mm	23–26
#3	Light (DK)	U.S. 5–7 3.75–4.5 mm	21–24
#4	Medium (worsted)	U.S. 7–9 4.5–5.5 mm	16–20
#5	Bulky (chunky)	U.S. 9–11 5.5–8 mm	12–15
#6	Super Bulky (bulky)	U.S. 11+ 8 mm+	6–11

The Skinny on Fine Yarns

We've said it before, and we'll say it again: Skinny yarns are underappreciated and underused. That bugs us, especially since some of our favorite yarns—some of the most luxurious and beautiful yarns, yarns that caress your hands as you knit with them, yarns that are handdyed in glorious colors, yarns that people wait in line for hours at fiber festivals to purchase—are thin yarns.

The three of us have logged some serious time working in a knitting shop. And one of the things we see over and over again is a mistrust of fine-gauge yarns. We've watched customers pick up a gorgeous skein of handdyed yarn, ask what weight the yarn is, then put the yarn back on the shelf like a pinless hand grenade when they hear "fingering weight." We've seen knitters drool over a particular pattern but balk when they find out that the pattern is written at a gauge of 6 or 7 stitches per inch. We've even heard someone who has been knitting for thirty years tell us that she's never used a yarn finer than worsted weight.

What gives? Why are so many knitters—experienced and newbie alike—afraid of fine yarns?

Obviously, there are a whole host of prejudices and misconceptions about skinny yarns. Place your right hand on a copy of *Knitting Without Tears* and swear to tell the truth, the whole truth, and nothing but the truth. Have you ever uttered any of the following sentiments?

"Skinny yarns take too long. I want to finish my sweater in this lifetime."
"Fine yarns are so . . . fiddly. I don't have the patience to fool around with them."
"I use fine yarns for lace and Fair Isle, but I'd never use them for an entire sweater."
"I knit to relax. Who wants to mess around with yarn that looks like dental floss and tangles at the drop of a hat?"

If you've said or thought anything along these lines, then pull up a chair, grab a mug of your favorite beverage, and be prepared to change your mind. We wrote this book for you. And we won't rest until we've convinced you that skinny yarns are . . . well . . . mighty fine.

Some of Our Favorite Skinny Yarns

We haven't met very many skinny yarns that we don't like. The list below includes some of our favorites.

- **BLACK BUNNY FIBERS LACE WEIGHT** (100% merino wool; 8+ stitches per inch). Lovely handdyed yarn for shawls and scarves.

- **BROWN SHEEP COTTON FINE** (80% cotton, 20% wool; 6½ stitches per inch). Versatile, well-priced, available in lots of colors.

- **HANDMAIDEN SEA SILK** (70% silk, 30% SeaCell; 7 stitches per inch). Another handdyed lovely for shawls and scarves.

- **JADE SAPPHIRE 2-PLY CASHMERE** (100% Mongolian cashmere; 6 to 8 stitches per inch). A combination of warmth, softness, and luxury.

- **JAGGERSPUN ZEPHYR** (50% tussah silk, 50% merino wool; 8+ stitches per inch). A great blend of fibers, a wide spectrum of colors, and lighter than light; you can't beat the softness, sheen, or value.

- **JAMIESON'S SHETLAND** (100% Shetland wool; 7 to 8 stitches per inch). Original, pure Shetland wool dyed in a nearly endless spectrum of colors; made specifically for Fair Isle knitting, but good for all kinds of shawls.

- **KOIGU KPPPM** (100% merino wool; 5½ to 8 stitches per inch). The colors, the twist, the way it looks great at a variety of gauges, the softness . . . and did we mention the colors? This handdyed merino is good for anything you can knit.

- **LORNA'S LACES HELEN'S LACE** (50% wool, 50% silk; 8+ stitches per inch). Handdyed yarn in variegated and nearly solid colors for shawls and scarves.

- **REGIA SILK** (55% wool, 25% polyamide, 20% silk; 7 stitches per inch). Designed for socks but versatile and luxurious enough for just about anything.

- **REYNOLDS SOFT SEA WOOL** (100% wool; 6½ to 7 stitches per inch). Another yarn designed for—but not limited to—socks, with a firm twist and great feel.

- **ROWAN KID SILK HAZE** (70% kid mohair, 30% silk; 6 stitches per inch). Dreamy colors, luscious hand, and light as snow. Knit it alone at 3 to 8 stitches per inch, as a carry-along with another yarn, or double-stranded for a less transparent look.

- **SCHAEFER ANNE** (60% merino wool, 25% mohair, 15% nylon; 7 to 8 stitches per inch). Scrumptious handdyed colors; works well whether knitted loosely for shawls or scarves or tightly for socks.

- **ZITRON TREKKING XXL** (75% wool, 25% nylon; 7 stitches per inch). A colorful sock yarn that's also great for other garments.

We think one of the best reasons to knit with fine yarns is the yarns themselves. We've listed some of our favorites on the facing page.

If you can resist picking up and fondling any of these yarns, you have a heart of stone, my friend. Why deny yourself the pleasure of knitting with such wonderful yarns?

But putting yarn lust aside, there are plenty of other reasons, practical and emotional, to knit with skinny yarns. Let's go through them one by one.

Better Fit

One of the most frustrating experiences a knitter can have is putting a lot of time and effort into a sweater, only to be dissatisfied with the way it fits. A thorough discussion of how to make your handknitted garments fit well would fill an entire book, but for now, suffice it to say that fine yarns offer greater opportunities to tweak the fit of a garment to your precise needs.

How can that be?

It's all those stitches and all those rows. The fact that you have more stitches per row and more rows per inch means you have that many more opportunities to increase a stitch here, or decrease one there, and then do it again a few rows later. If you need to nip in a sweater at the waist by just a half inch, and you're

knitting at, say, 8 stitches to an inch, you can decrease 4 stitches and the sweater will hit you at exactly the right spot. In contrast, if your yarn knits up at 3 stitches per inch, you'd be stuck with a slightly larger decrease (⅔ inch) or a slightly smaller decrease (⅓ inch). Greater precision means greater fit—and that's where skinny yarns can be your best friends.

Achieving good fit with your knitwear is a topic that's beyond the scope of this book, but it's important to summarize some of the key points.

◎ Take accurate, honest measurements with a cloth measuring tape.

◎ Study the schematic of the garment you plan to make before you cast on, paying special attention to the structure of the sleeves, armhole depth, and overall length to familiarize yourself with the dimensions and construction.

Even the fashion doll—with her exaggerated proportions—looks better in the clingy, thin, curve-hugging fine-gauge yarn.

◎ Pay close attention to your gauge and recheck it several times as you knit each piece.

◎ If you're uncertain about which size to knit, measure the width and length of a garment that fits you the way you'd like your project to fit you, then use those measurements as a frame of reference for choosing a size to knit.

◎ Consider the amount of ease you want in the finished garment.

◎ Check out the Bibliography on page 142 for some great references on fit and garment construction.

Flattery

The better a garment fits, the more flattering it looks. And because you can get a better fit with finer yarn, you'll look best in fine-gauge sweaters.

But apart from precision fitting, the inherent nature of thin yarns—their, well, thinness—means that they add less bulk to the wearer. Look at the photos above of a 14-inch fashion doll wearing a simple dress made of a yarn that knits at 3 stitches per inch and the same doll wearing a similar tube dress made of a yarn that knits at 7 stitches per inch. Even the fashion doll—with her

The dress on the left was knitted with bulky yarn at 3 stitches per inch; the dress on the right was knitted with a fine yarn at 7 stitches per inch.

freakishly exaggerated proportions—looks better in the clingy, thin, curve-hugging fine-gauge yarn. If the difference in gauge makes a doll look better, imagine what it will do for real bodies!

You also want to think about the seams. Although knitting in the round is a wonderful technique, it isn't possible (or practical) with every pattern, and seams are sometimes necessary to provide structure in a garment. Seams sewn with chunky yarns will be considerably thicker and bulkier than those with fine yarns. A thick and bulky seam adds lumps and bumps, and who needs those?

You'll find fine yarns particularly flattering if you happen to be a woman who wears a plus-size. As Jillian Moreno and Amy Singer (authors of *Big Girl Knits*; Potter Craft, 2006) so aptly put it:

> *Big Girls Knits should use yarn four stitches to the inch or finer, period. Do not put bulky, super-chunky-monkey garments on your big girl body. Thick yarn doesn't add inches to your silhouette, it adds feet.*

Fine-gauge yarns are also an excellent choice for petite women. Thicker, bulkier yarns and garments may overwhelm a small frame. Finer yarns will provide a more proportionate look for women with diminutive statures or small bone structures.

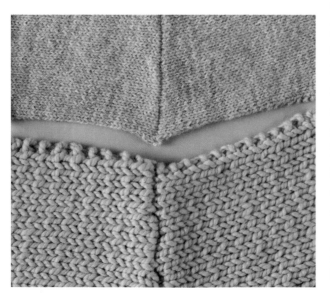

A seam sewn in a fabric knitted with fine yarn (top) is smoother and less bulky than a seam sewn in fabric knitted with bulky yarn (bottom).

Feel

Feel is, of course, a totally subjective element. And don't get us wrong: There is something satisfying and cozy about snuggling into a thick wool sweater . . . if you have the luxury of lying around, in a cool room, in a climate where you get temperatures that dip below 10 degrees Fahrenheit on a regular basis.

On the other hand, if you live in a climate like ours—we live in Philadelphia, where winters aren't terribly cold and summers are hot and humid—you don't spend a lot of time wrapped up in thick wool. Indeed, you can't spend much time wrapped up in a burly sweater without feeling sweaty and uncomfortable.

And this leads us to a big advantage of thin yarns: They are lightweight. By definition, thin yarns weigh less than thick ones because they contain less wool or alpaca or cotton or whatever fiber they're made from. Less weight and less fiber mean less perspiration. It means you can wear your beautifully crafted garment more days of the year—from September through May instead of a handful of days in January and February. Don't make the mistake of thinking that cotton, a fiber that is inherently cooler than wool, will be more comfortable in a heavyweight sweater. Cotton may be cooler to wear than wool, but it's heavier. Way, way

A lace pattern looks better when knitted in a fine yarn.

Only with a lightweight yarn can you achieve the ethereal, cobweb effect of lace designs.

Fine Yarns Do What Thick Ones Can't

Consider the following handknitted items: a lace shawl, a twin set, a pair of socks, a summer top, a cabled hat, an intarsia sweater, a Fair Isle cardigan. These seemingly diverse handknits have one thing in common: Because they're all knitted out of fine yarns, they achieve effects that items knitted from thick yarns can't.

LACE SHAWL | Lace shawls can, of course, be knitted in yarns of varying thickness. But the difference between a shawl knitted in a fine yarn— fingering, laceweight, even sportweight—and one knitted in a thicker yarn is striking. The design shows to maximum effect with a thin yarn—only with a lightweight yarn can you achieve the ethereal, cobweb effect of lace designs. Consider that shawls are designed as layering pieces and you'll realize that you'll have many more chances to wear an airy, lightweight shawl than a heavy, hot one made of thick wool.

TWIN SET | We bet you've never seen a twin set knitted in a yarn thicker than DK weight. The essence of the twin set is layering—impossible as a practical matter with thick yarns. Any garment designed to be worn as a layer—whether a delicate camisole with lace

heavier. A lightweight cotton sweater will be more comfortable to wear simply because it weighs less.

And wearability isn't restricted to climate. If you move around during the course of a day (in our "normal" days we lug groceries, carry children, schlep boxes, reach for books on high shelves, and a whole lot more), a thinner, less bulky garment is infinitely more comfortable. Most women have busy, active lives, and prefer clothing that doesn't constrict or slow them down. Try on a fine-gauge sweater and you'll see what we mean. You won't waddle like a penguin on an iceberg, constricted by thick layers of fabric and awkward seams. Instead, you'll glide like Audrey Hepburn through the doorway of Tiffany's.

trim or a vintage 1950s twin set—has to be thin to be wearable.

SOCKS | Socks can be knitted in heavy yarns, in which case they're labeled "boot" or "bed" socks. Not that there's anything wrong with a thick, cozy pair of socks. But unless you wear a lightweight sock made of thin yarn, you'll never be able to shoehorn your foot into your favorite loafers. Comfort and fit (not to mention avoiding excessively sweaty, stinky feet) require that you use a lightweight yarn (one that knits up at 7 or more stitches to the inch) to make a pair of socks that will fit comfortably in most shoes.

SUMMER TOP | Yep, you can see where this one's going. Summer = hot, and that means the lighter the fabric, the cooler you'll be. 'Nuff said.

CABLE-PATTERNED CAP | Knitting at a fine gauge means you'll have more stitches per horizontal inch and more rows per vertical inch. That means you'll have more pattern repeats, too. Some stitch patterns have long repeats—flip through a stitch treasury like any of the ones by Barbara Walker and you'll find that many stitch patterns repeat over 10 or more stitches

and 8 or more rows. Because the stitches are smaller with fine-gauge yarns, you'll be able to work more pattern repeats, both horizontally and vertically.

If you're knitting a small item such as a hat, you may find that a single, lengthy stitch pattern won't even fit around the circumference. You certainly won't be able to use many repeats, and you may distort the size if you add stitches to complete a repeat. Simply put, finer-gauge yarns give you access to a greater selection of stitch or color patterns.

You'll be able to fit in more cable repeats (both horizontally and vertically) by using thin yarns instead of thick yarns.

COLOR WORK | Intarsia and Fair Isle are two methods that use multiple colors of yarn. Intarsia involves knitting isolated blocks of colors, with a separate ball of yarn for each color block. The colors are twisted around each other at the color changes. What we loosely term "Fair Isle" involves any method of working with two or more colors in a row, carrying (or stranding) the unused color(s) along the back of the work.

Both of these techniques add bulk and lumpiness to a garment from the twisted or stranded yarns—something that can be unsightly in a bulky yarn but isn't noticeable in a fine one. If that's not bad enough, the weight of heavy yarn strands can pull and distort the stitches and the color pattern. That's why so many color-work masterpieces are worked in fingering–, sport–, or DK weight yarn.

Retro and Vintage Styling

If you like vintage or retro styles, you'll want to be comfortable working with fine yarns. A quick skim through older knitwear magazines (and by older, we mean pre-1950s, before mass-produced sweaters and man-made fibers became prevalent) shows that gauges of 7, 8, or more stitches to the inch were common. To re-create the true vintage look, you'll need to use fine yarn and needles, just like the originals.

Even if you're comfortable rewriting patterns for a thicker yarn with a different gauge, you may be surprised at how difficult it can be to translate vintage patterns into heavier yarns. For example, many of the beautifully tailored effects of vintage knits—nipped-in waists and close-fitting set-in sleeves—are difficult to achieve with thick yarns. As we've already mentioned, many intricate patterns (such as those used in vintage

Length of Stitch Pattern in Fine versus Thick Yarn

Suppose you want to knit a hat with a finished circumference of 20 inches in a stitch pattern that repeats over 28 stitches and 20 rows. If you chose a thick yarn that knits up at 2 stitches per inch, you'd have trouble fitting two full repeats of the stitch pattern in the hat's circumference. One pattern repeat would require 28 stitches; two repeats would require 56 stitches. At this gauge, that would translate to a finished circumference of 14 inches—too small for an adult—or a whopping 28 inches—too big for a watermelon. And we haven't even considered whether the large row gauge (maybe 2 or 3 rows per inch) would accommodate the 20-row repeat. But if you used fingering-weight wool at 7 stitches per inch, you'd be able to fit five full pattern repeats into the desired circumference.

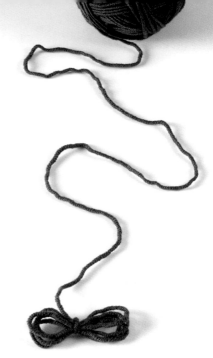

designs) won't work at thick-yarn gauges. And even if you can surmount these practical problems, you'll likely find that when worked in a heavier yarn, your garment will lose some of the intangible appeal of the original.

Take a walk through a yard sale or your local flea market, or use an online auction site to find vintage knitting magazines for some lovely patterns that were published in bygone days. Or look at some of the books based on vintage fashions that have been published recently—some of them are listed in the Bibliography on page 142.

As Jane Waller, who has written several books devoted to vintage handknitting, cautions modern knitters:

> *"Authentic 1940s garments were made from pure wools in a fine ply on fine needles and made to last. . . . [If] you use too thick a yarn, you will lose that particularly soft, fine-textured look that is typical of the period."*

The special appeal of certain vintage items—lightness, softness, shapeliness—is due in no small measure to their reliance on light, soft, and yes, fine yarns.

Traditional and Ethnic History

Handknitting has a tremendously rich and varied history. Again, exploring even a fraction of this history goes well beyond the scope of this book, but it seems as though as long as people have been knitting, they've been thinking up ways to make their knitting beautiful, obscuring the boundary between art and craft. Some of our favorite areas of traditional and ethnic knitting include Shetland lace, the stranded knitting of the northern islands of Britain and of Scandinavia, the Swedish Bohus tradition, Germanic traveling stitches, Andean folk knitting, Turkish stranded knitting, and Eastern European traditions (particularly Latvian and Estonian). Interestingly, many traditional or ethnic styles of knitting are done using skinny yarns in reaction to bulk, distortion, heaviness, and scarcity of wool.

Recent years have seen a resurgence of interest in ethnic and traditional knitting, so you'll find many wonderful books devoted to specific folk knitting traditions. Check out the Bibliography for some of our favorites.

Yarn that is twisted more tightly tends to wear better than yarn that is loosely spun.

Economics

All other things being equal, it's more economical to knit sweaters using skinny yarns than it is using thicker ones. Don't believe us? Take it from Elizabeth Zimmerman (*Knitting Without Tears*; Fireside/Simon & Schuster, 1995):

> *If you prefer to economize and love to knit, make your sweaters with very fine wool and many stitches. A thin sweater weighs much less than a great heavy one, and, broadly speaking, wool sells by weight. Fine knitting gives you many more hours of your favorite hobby before you have to sally forth and make another capital investment.*

In other words, knitting with fine yarns saves you money in two ways: the yarn costs less, and you get more hours of enjoyment from the money you spend on yarn for each project. Here's how:

Suppose you knit a simple sweater with a 36-inch circumference and set-in sleeves. Using Karabella's Aurora as our example (since this yarn comes in varying weights), you'd need about 725 yards of Aurora Bulky (3½ stitches per inch); 950 yards of Karabella 8 (4½ stitches per inch); or 1,590 yards of Aurora 4 (7 stitches per inch). The cost (at the time of this writing) would be about $97 for Bulky (12.95 balls at $7.50 per

Bulky yarns, which are often loosely spun, don't wear as well as fine yarns that are tightly plied.

56-yard ball), $72.70 for Aran weight (9.7 balls at $7.50 per 98-yard ball), and $64.57 for fingering weight (8.07 balls at $8 per 197-yard ball). How about that? You'd save over thirty bucks by using the fingering-weight yarn!

Another way to compare the economics is to look at the cost per hour of your knitting enjoyment. Using the example above, a knitter would spend about $97 for a bulky wool, and it would take her, say, 50 hours to knit the sweater. Divide 97 dollars by 50 hours, and you get a "cost" of $1.94 per hour. Now, if that same knitter used fingering-weight wool, she'd spend $64.57 on the yarn and about 125 hours to knit the sweater. Divide 64.57 by 125 hours and you'll see that it costs her just 52 cents per hour of enjoyment.

Now think about all of this in terms of luxury fiber. A bulky-weight pure cashmere yarn (for example, Classic Elite's Sinful) costs, at the time of this writing, a whopping $49 dollars for a 65-yard ball. You'd need about 725 yards to make an average size 36 sweater, for a total cost of $546.35. But if you use fine-gauge cashmere instead, like Karabella Super Cashmere at $23 per 202 yards, the total cost is substantially less even though you'd need more yards of yarn—1,590 yards would cost $179.40. You'd end up with a cashmere sweater for $360 less. And a more affordable cashmere sweater can only be described as A Very Good Thing.

Durability

We don't have any scientific proof, but we believe that fine yarns, as a rule, wear better than heavier yarns. In thinking about it, we've come up with some possible explanations.

With less yarn and thinner fabric, we suspect that there will be less friction. Friction, the rubbing of the fabric against itself or another object, leads to wear and possibly pilling.

Another explanation has to do with the way yarns are spun at the mill. Oftentimes, very thick yarns are made of one strand (single ply), instead of multiple plies, and the fibers in these yarns are often spun together loosely. Yarn that is twisted more tightly tends to wear better than yarn that is loosely spun. But tightly spun yarns don't have to be hard and coarse—fine-gauge yarns can be more tightly spun or use multiple plies without losing their softness.

Experience from our sock-knitting days also factors into our theory. Most hardcore sock knitters knit at a gauge of 7, 8, or more stitches per inch. The conventional wisdom among sock knitters is that the tighter the stitches and the more of them packed together per square inch, the less each individual stitch will wear and the longer the socks will last. We can't think of a single reason why this wouldn't hold true for larger garments as well.

Dazzling Results

If you have any lingering doubts, we hope that a quick flip through the patterns in the rest of this book will persuade you that fine-gauge yarns are worth getting to know.

Tips, Tools, and Techniques

As with any project, getting set up with the right tools and knowing the tricks of the trade can help immeasurably when knitting. We want your fine-gauge experience to go as smoothly as possible, so refrain from casting on just a little longer while you review the following technical tips. Many of them are applicable to your knitting no matter how thick or thin the yarn is; others are particularly helpful with thinner yarns.

Yarn Selection

We're going to assume for now that you understand the concept of gauge and yarn weight enough to select a yarn that's appropriate for the project you have in mind (or that you can avail yourself of the wisdom of the friendly folks at your local yarn shop to help you if you don't). We'll talk more about gauge later—believe us; we will—but in the meantime, let's talk yarn.

If you feel some trepidation about the transition from thick yarns to thin, take it easy on yourself and consider working with a yarn that isn't drastically different from what you're used to. Look for projects that use yarn with a gauge of 5½ or 6 stitches per inch instead of 7 or more. You'll still see the advantages of a finer yarn but the change in yarn and needle size won't be as dramatic. If change intimidates you, then ease into it.

COLOR | Follow the advice we regularly give newbie knitters when it comes to picking yarns. Chose a light-colored yarn—it's easier to work with because the stitches show up more clearly in light than dark colors. Likewise, the stitches are easier to see in solid-colored yarns than variegated or handpainted ones. And stay away from yarns that are fuzzy or hairy (like mohair, which is known for its "halo" of long fibers). The long fibers in these yarns can obscure the stitches and because they tend to catch on one another, they make it difficult to rip without breaking or knotting. Finally, avoid novelty or other yarns that have inconsistencies in thickness or spin. Your best bet is to start with a smooth, consistently spun yarn. Not only will you find these yarns glide smoothly along your fingers, you'll get more even tension and the individual stitches will show up clearly so you'll notice mistakes as soon as you make them, not after the sweater is off the needles.

Yarn Selection and Substitution

Beginning knitters are often told that they can substitute different yarns for the one called for in the pattern as long as the substitute yarn will get the same gauge as the original. Technically, this is true. But if gauge compatibility is all you consider, your results may be very, very different from the original. To make a successful substitution, you need to consider the characteristics of the fabric, the yarn, and the fiber.

Cabled Vest

Drapey Silk Top

◉ DRAPE The Drapey Silk Top (page 36) and the Cabled Vest (page 44) are both knitted at the same gauge. But one is supple and slinky, while the other is dense and sturdy. The "drape" of a fabric depends on several things: fiber (silk is inherently drapier than wool; wool is inherently bouncier—more elastic—than silk), yarn structure (more tightly spun yarns produce denser fabrics than loosely spun yarns), knitting tension (the same yarn will yield a softer, drapier fabric when knitted on bigger needles than on smaller needles), and stitch pattern (cable patterns produce denser fabrics; lace patterns produce looser ones).

Fabrics with lots of drape move easily with the body, and they often look dressier or sexier than garments knitted with more body. But there are tradeoffs: Drapey fabrics are more prone to sag and stretch out of shape.

◉ FIBER CONTENT Among the plant fibers, soy and bamboo are generally drapier than cotton or linen; of these, linen holds its shape best. Among the protein fibers, alpaca and cashmere usually have softer drape than wool, partly because of their fiber structure and partly because, being both warm and expensive, they're often spun to a finer gauge than wool. (Finer-gauge yarn = drapier fabric.) On the other hand, mohair and wool both produce fabrics with better memory.

As with so many things in knitting, none of these is "better" than the others—any one can be the best yarn for your purpose in any given project.

FIBER CONTENT | Next, give some thought to the fiber in your prospective yarn. Different fibers have different characteristics: Wool is resilient and elastic, cotton and silk are inelastic. Silk and rayon are smooth and slippery. If you have joint pain in your hands or repetitive-motion injuries, consider using a wool or wool-blend yarn. Because it is bouncy and elastic, wool is easier on your hands than most fibers. Remember, many of the advantages of fine yarn stem from the fact that there are more stitches and more rows of knitting involved, so you'll want to be sure to choose a fiber that will minimize aching hands or wrists.

SWATCHING | Our last tip is one that knitters rarely like to hear, but it's essential: Knit a larger-than-usual gauge swatch. Buy a single ball of your prospective yarn and knit yourself a jumbo (at least 8 inches by 8 inches) square with it. Accurate gauge measurements are critical if you want a sweater to fit, but beyond that crucial consideration, it helps to know exactly what you're working with. You'll get to know the yarn while you swatch with it—you'll learn how it feels in your hands and behaves on the needles. Experiment with different types of needles to see which one maximizes your knitting enjoyment. And as a practical matter, a good-size swatch can help you head off any future dissatisfaction with your yarn choice. We've all been taken in by yarns that look appealing in the hank but are maybe a bit disappointing (or downright annoying) on the needles. You'll be working with this yarn for a while, so make

sure you love it before you invest any more time or money in it, or choose a different yarn that you do love.

No Tangles, Please

All yarn has a tendency to tangle if not handled carefully. A simple way to head off tangles is to carry only the ball that you're working with in your knitting bag—store the others elsewhere so they can't get tangled up with the work in progress. Another trick is to use some sort of cover over the ball to keep it intact. You can find such covers at yarn shops (one is called the "Yarn Bra") or you can make your own out of a knee-high stocking (tuck the ball inside the knee-high and feed the working end out the top) or a zippper-top bag (place the ball in the bag and close the zipper until just the working end has room to thread through). Opinions differ about the center-pull ball (a ball of yarn wound so that the working end pulls from the

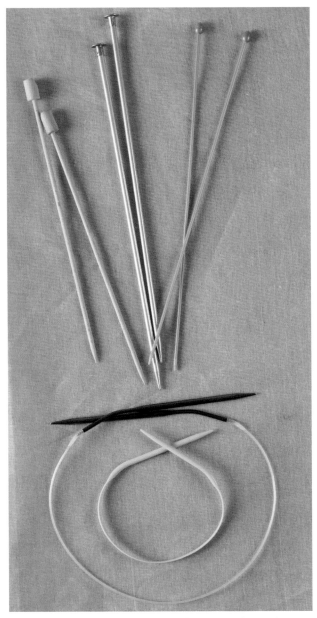

There are dozens of needles to choose from—straight, circular, wood, metal, and plastic are some of the most common.

center of the ball rather than the outside). Many knitters swear center-pull balls head off tangles; others find that the ball collapses on itself after the core of yarn has been used. If a center-pull ball does look in imminent danger of collapse, rewind the yarn into a "normal" ball, beginning with the outside end. Remember that balls wound from some yarns, especially smooth, slippery ones like silk, rayon, and ribbon tend to slide apart, leading to more tangles. You may find it helpful to wind these yarns around a rectangle of cardboard instead of working directly from the balls.

Needles

The type of knitting needles you use is largely a matter of choice; you probably already have your own preferences and favorites. Many knitters have strong feelings about the type of needle they prefer. Each opinion is valid: No type of needle is "better" than another. Straight, circular, wooden, metal, blunt- or sharp-tipped—try them all to see which appeal to you.

STRAIGHT NEEDLES have a traditional feel, leave no chance for accidentally joining work into a tube, are clearly marked with the needle size, and are preferred (especially by some tight knitters) because they have no "bump" to snag the yarn.

CIRCULAR NEEDLES work well in confined spaces, offer the versatility of working "flat" or "in the round," accommodate large numbers of stitches, and pass airport security more easily than straight needles.

WOODEN AND/OR BAMBOO NEEDLES are warm to the touch, may have beautifully worked end-knobs, "grip" slippery yarns, and pass airport security more easily than metal needles.

METAL NEEDLES are very durable, allow sticky yarns to "slip," and allow stitches to slide more easily (an advantage for tight knitters and those in a hurry).

BLUNT-TIPPED NEEDLES present less risk of injury, are less likely to split thicker or denser yarns, and are less likely to snag small loops (as in bouclé or other textured yarns).

SHARP-TIPPED NEEDLES offer greater precision for fine-gauge work, penetrate tight stitches more easily, and facilitate the stitch manipulations required for many textured patterns.

Keep in mind that the material or coating of the needle can affect how quickly yarn slides over them. Slick metal coatings, like the nickel that covers Addi Turbo needles, are designed to let the yarn slide over the needle quickly. If you're interested in speed, this is the needle for you. If you find the speed dizzying, or you're using a slippery yarn like pure silk, try wood or bamboo needles, which have more porous surfaces that "grip" the yarn and stitches.

If you're looking for a circular needle, opt for a smooth join—the junction between the cable and the needle tip. Stitches will catch on a rough or bulky join, and you'll constantly have to wiggle the stitches over it. On the other hand, a smooth join (we love the ones on Addi Turbos) allow the stitches to slide "seamlessly" around the needle.

There are lots of types of stitch markers; some fit around knitting needles, others hook onto individual stitches.

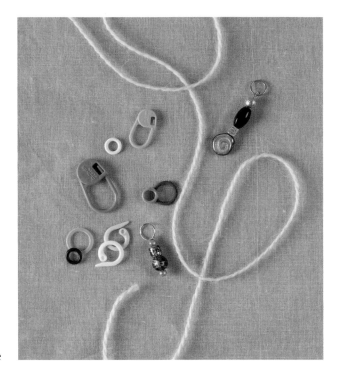

In addition to allowing for knitting in rounds, circular needles distribute large numbers of stitches over the entire lengths of their cables, and all of those stitches (and the knitting connected to them) fall comfortably into the knitter's lap. Circular needles come in different lengths, from scant 12 inches to 40 inches or longer. The longer the needle, the more stitches it can hold. The sizes for circular needles involve two measurements—one to represent the diameter of the needle (just like straight needles) and the other to indicate the length of the cable between the two needle tips. Sometimes the length of the cable won't matter much (i.e., you can knit a sweater in the round on a circular with a 24-inch cable as easily as a 29-inch cable), but other times you'll need a particular length (such as a 16-inch cable for knitting necklines in the round).

Different brands of needles have slightly different points. Though they're subtle, you can see the differences if you look closely, or you may be able to feel the difference when you knit. Many knitters prefer sharper points when working with fine yarns or with stitch patterns that involve a lot of decreases or cables. Sharp points slide into the stitches more easily than blunt ones, but if you knit in such a way that your fingertips frequently rub the tips of the needles, you may find sharp tips painful after knitting for a while.

The Versatile Stitch Marker

There are all sorts of stitch markers—some are wafer-thin while others are thick and chubby; some are continuous rings while others have a split or opening; and some are plain while others are decorated with beads and doodads. Whatever type you like, don't forget that you can use them for a lot more than marking the beginning of rounds in circular knitting.

MARK SECTIONS OF A GARMENT | When you're knitting a sweater in the round, use stitch markers on the needles to denote the position of each side "seam." This will help you keep track of the front and back. When knitting a pattern that calls for a series of aligned decreases (as in the Lace-Trimmed Raglan on page 78) or increases, use markers to denote where to work them. Instead of counting stitches, you'll know to work a decrease (or increase) when you come to the marker.

DENOTE SEPARATE STITCH PATTERNS |
Use stitch markers on the needles to denote the boundaries between separate stitch patterns. For example, the Lace-Trimmed Raglan has a vertical panel of lace along the stockinette-stitch sleeves. A marker before the first stitch and another marker after the last stitch of the lace motif will alert you when it's time to switch between the stockinette and lace patterns.

KEEP TRACK OF PATTERN REPEATS | If there
are multiple repeats of the same pattern in a row of knitting, try placing stitch markers on the needles after every few repeats. That way, you'll break the row into smaller sections, and you'll quickly learn the sequence of stitches that come before each marker (knit 1, purl 2, for example), and you'll know right away that you've made a mistake if you have a different type of stitch (knit 1, purl 1, for example) before the next marker. Not only will you notice your mistake before the end of the row, you'll only have to rip out to the previous marker.

KEEP TRACK OF INCREASES AND DECREASES |
To keep track of the number of increases or decreases worked in a series (such as "increase/decrease 1 stitch each end of needle every 4th row 8 times"), place an open-ring marker (the kind that has an opening or looks like a coilless safety pin) in a stitch at each end of every row that involves an increase or a decrease. This will make it easy to keep track of the number of shaping rows completed and, if you leave the markers in place, you can use them to match up the pieces when sewing seams later.

If your pattern requires you to decrease a particular number of stitches (such as 1 stitch on the next 10 right-side rows) place a marker on the needle before the first stitch to be decreased and after the last stitch to be decreased. You'll know you've worked all the decreases when the markers meet. Similarly, you can also use this technique to set off certain types of increases.

USE COLORS TO YOUR ADVANTAGE |
Use different-colored markers to alert you to different things. For example, use a red marker to denote the beginning of the round, blue markers to set apart stitch patterns, and yellow markers to denote lines of increases and decreases. Create your own visual code for your next project.

Other Necessities

Although each knitter has favorite tips and tricks for successful knitting, we think the following are invaluable for preventing mistakes and ensuring good results.

POINT PROTECTORS | Point protectors are small rubber or plastic caps that fit on the tips of needles to prevent stitches from sliding off. They are invaluable for ensuring that the stitches stay on the needles when you're not knitting. Keep a couple of point protectors with your knitting to prevent potential heartbreak when your knitting time is interrupted.

LIGHTING | Give yourself every advantage you can. Knit in good light. Your eyes—and your knitting—will thank you.

TRIAL RUNS | Before you cast on stitches for an entire sweater, practice a new or challenging stitch pattern in a swatch. With a smooth, light-colored yarn, cast on enough stitches for a few widthwise repeats of the pattern, then knit a few repeats vertically. You'll learn the ins and outs of the pattern without worrying about ripping out dozens (or hundreds) of stitches when you make mistakes. By the time you've mastered a few repeats, you'll know how the stitches relate to each other, and you'll be ready to cast on for your project.

LIFELINES | If you're worried about making mistakes and having to rip out rows and rows of knitting, take a tip from hardcore lace knitters and use a lifeline. A lifeline is a length of smooth, thin yarn or thread that is threaded through an entire row of stitches. It holds the stitches (and yarnovers) in order and in the correct orientation so that if you find a mistake on a subsequent row, you can pull out the needles, rip down to the lifeline, then use the lifeline as a guide for placing the stitches back on the needles properly. To insert a lifeline, thread a length of fine, smooth cotton yarn (or sewing thread, dental floss, or embroidery

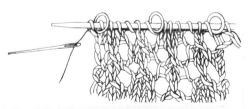

Thread the lifeline through the stitches at the base of the knitting needle.

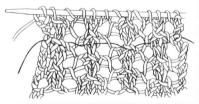

Continue to work as usual.

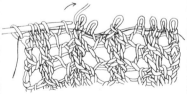

If you need to rip out, use the lifeline as a guide for putting the stitches on the needle correctly.

floss) through the stitches (but not the markers, if there are any) along the base of the knitting needle. It's easiest, but not necessary, to insert the lifeline in a plain row, such as an all-knit or all-purl row. Tie the ends of the lifeline together to secure it, then continue knitting as usual. Some knitters insert lifelines every few inches so they never have far to rip out. Lifelines are most commonly used with lace patterns, but there's no reason not to use them other times—if your stitches are tiny, your stitch pattern is complex, your yarn is fuzzy and the stitches are hard to see, or whenever you want a little knitting insurance.

Finishing

Don't rush the finishing process, no matter how impatient you are to be done. Hear us? Do not rush through your finishing. Make sure you are well-rested (under no circumstances should you hurry to finish a garment at midnight just so you can wear it to a fiber festival the next day) and always work under good light. Carol is compulsive about her finishing. To make sure that she doesn't go too fast and get sloppy, she limits herself to sewing just one seam a day. Because she doesn't expect to be done quickly, she takes time to review the seam sewn the previous day before she starts the next one. While Carol's approach may seem extreme, her results are always professional. So take your time and keep an open mind towards ripping out and resewing if necessary. After working so

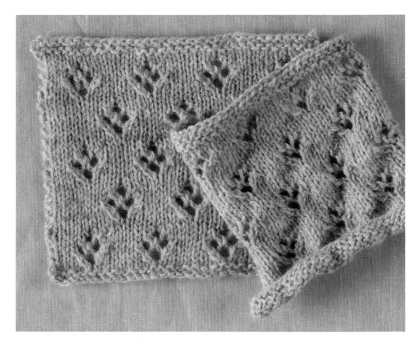

Blocking evens out the stitches and gives a finished look to any piece of knitting.

diligently on a garment, you don't want to spoil it with sloppy seams.

And finally, remember to block the finished pieces. Blocking is the single most important thing that a knitter can do to improve the quality of finished knitwear. And because garments knitted in fine yarns take longer to complete, there's more opportunity for variances in individual stitches and more stitches and rows that need to look even. Give the pieces a good steaming or soak them in cool water (be guided by the yarn label, which should specify washability), then pin them to shape. For the best results, use blocking wires (available at knitting shops) to shape the pieces without telltale pin marks.

These swatches are knitted with the same yarn, needles, and number of stitches, but they were knitted by two different people. This shows how gauge can vary between knitters.

Gauge

You thought we might forget about it, didn't you? And you know what we're going to say, don't you? Always knit a gauge swatch.

We'll repeat it, anyway: Always knit a gauge swatch. *Always.*

Making sure that you get the right number of stitches per inch and rows per inch is always crucial if you want garments that fit and look like they're supposed to. This is even more important when working with skinny yarns. You're going to put more time into knitting your garment simply because there are more stitches. You don't want to waste any of that energy on a sweater that is too big or too small.

As important as it is to determine your gauge before you cast on stitches, it's equally important to recheck your gauge periodically as you knit. It's possible that your gauge may change somewhat as you get used to the yarn or as you change from being relaxed to being tense. It's far better to notice and correct these problems before you bind off the last stitch.

As important as it is to determine your gauge before you cast on stitches, it's equally important to recheck your gauge periodically as you knit.

Staying Motivated

Of all the reasons knitters give for not using fine yarns, we most commonly hear that they don't want to spend so much time on a single project. We live in a world of instant gratification, and even knitters have grown accustomed to projects that are "quick-knits" or that can be finished in a weekend. While there are some projects that knit up quickly in fine yarn, the fact of the matter is that most projects are going to take, well, a while. If you're afraid you'll poop out before your sweater is finished, try some of these tricks to keep yourself knitting:

◎ Alternate a fine-gauge project with a quick-knit one. Whipping out some caps or scarves will help satisfy your need for accomplishment.

◎ Take time to knit at least a few rows every day. Whether you use knitting as time for quiet relaxation or while listening to music or watching your favorite TV show, allow time to enjoy it daily.

◎ When knitting large pieces, such as sweater fronts or backs, measure your progress every few days, not every few hours. It takes time to make progress with fine yarn, and you may only depress yourself if you find that you've added a mere half inch since you last measured.

◎ Join a knit-along or write a blog about your sweater progress.

◎ Set small goals such as finishing a cuff or working two inches instead of always looking to when the project will be finished. Try writing these goals on a piece of paper and crossing them off as they're accomplished.

◎ Find a knitting buddy and arrange times to get together to knit and encourage each other.

◎ Treat yourself to a small pleasure when you reach particular milestones—an ice cream cone when you finish the sleeve, a new CD when the front and back are done, or a ball of sock yarn when you're ready to block.

Now that you're full of information, tricks, and techniques, it's time to turn to the fun part—the patterns.

Simplicity

Many of the knitting techniques traditionally worked in fine yarns—such as Shetland lace, Norwegian ski sweaters, and Swedish Bohus sweaters—are intricate and complex. Small wonder that many knitters think they could never knit a gorgeous Fair Isle jumper in thirty shades of fingering-weight yarn. We think you can, especially if you take it slow and start at the very beginning.

You can take advantage of many of the special qualities and techniques of fine yarns without using fifty-odd colors of Shetland wool or following pages of detailed charts. This section is devoted to the first steps: manageable projects that teach the basics of working with thinner yarns and smaller needles than you may be used to. You'll gain confidence as you work these projects, and we wager you'll be so pleased with the results that you'll come back for more.

Projects

Ruffle Scarf

Drapey Silk Top

Cowlneck Pullover

Cabled Vest

Kimono Top

Ruffle Scarf

CAROL SULCOSKI

This soft and feminine scarf is knitted lengthwise in cool shades of blue and is adorned with vertical rows of eyelets and mohair/silk ruffles on the long edges. By knitting the scarf the long way, it's easy to create vertical stripes. Don't be intimidated by the number of stitches—you'll knit far fewer rows to make up for it!

Scarf Center

With MC and larger needle, CO 336 sts. Do not join for working in rnds. Working back and forth in rows, knit every row until piece measures ¾" (2 cm) from CO. Change to 2 strands of CC1 held tog and smaller needle and knit 2 rows. **Next row:** Sl 1, *p2tog, yo; rep from * to last st, p1. Rep this row once more. Knit 2 rows even. Change to MC and larger needle and knit every row until piece measures ¾" (2 cm) from color change. Change to 2 strands of CC1 held tog and smaller needle and knit 2 rows. **Next row:** Sl 1, *p2tog, yo; rep from * to last st, p1. Rep this row once more. Knit 2 rows even. Change to MC and larger needle and knit every row until piece measures ¾" (2 cm) from color change. BO all sts.

Ruffle

With smaller needle, CC3, RS facing, and beg at CO (long) edge, pick up and knit 1 st in back loop of each CO st of scarf center—336 sts. Change to larger needle and work as foll:
Row 1: (WS) Knit.
Row 2: (RS) K1, k1f&b in every st to last st, k1—670 sts.
Row 3: Knit.
Row 4: Rep Row 2—1,338 sts.
Knit every row until ruffle measures 1" (2.5 cm) from pick-up row, ending with a RS row. BO all sts knitwise.
Rep for BO edge of scarf center.

Finishing

Weave in loose ends.

Finished Size About 5" (12.5 cm) wide and 60" (152.5 cm) long.

Yarn Fingering weight (#1 Super Fine) for MC; laceweight for CC1 and CC2.
Shown here: Rowan Cashsoft 4-Ply (57% wool, 33% microfiber, 10% cashmere; 197 yd [180 m]/50 g): #424 Spa (MC), 2 balls. Jaggerspun Zephyr (50% merino, 50% tussah silk; 630 yd [576 m]/2 oz): Ice Blue (CC1), 2 balls.
Rowan Kid Silk Haze (70% super kid mohair, 30% silk; 229 yd [209 m]/25 g): #592 heavenly (CC2), 2 balls.

Needles U.S. sizes 3 and 2 (3.25 and 2.75 mm): 24" (60 cm) circular (cir). Adjust needle size if necessary to obtain the correct gauge.

Notions Tapestry needle.

Gauge 22 stitches and 44 rows = 4" (10 cm) in garter stitch with MC on larger needles.

Drapey Silk Top

CAROL SULCOSKI

One of the many advantages of fine yarn is the way it can create fabrics with lots of drape—especially when that yarn is made of 100% silk. The loose crossover fronts accentuate the luxurious drape while the twisted rib edging hugs the waist. Wear this simple vest over a slinky dress for special occasions or pair it with a T-shirt and jeans for everyday wear.

Finished Size 32 (36, 40, 44)" (81.5 [91.5, 101.5, 112] cm) bust circumference. Top shown measures 36" (91.5 cm). To fit bust size 30–32 (34–36, 38–40, 42–44)" (71–81.5 [86.5–91.5, 96.5–101.5, 106.5–12] cm).

Yarn Sportweight (#2 Fine). *Shown here:* Colinette Tao (100% silk; 126 yd [115 m]/50 g): moss, 5 (5, 6, 7) skeins.

Needles Body—U.S. size 6 (4 mm). Edging—U.S. size 4 (3.5 mm): straight and 16" (40 cm) circular (cir). Adjust needle size if necessary to obtain the correct gauge.

Notions Markers (m); stitch holders or waste yarn; tapestry needle.

Gauge 24 stitches and 34 rows = 4" (10 cm) in stockinette stitch on larger needles.

Stitch Guide
Moss Stitch (worked in rounds)
Rnd 1: *K1, p1; rep from * to end of rnd.
Rnd 2: *P1, k1; rep from * to end of rnd.
Rep Rounds 1 and 2 for pattern.

Notes
◎ The asymmetric front features a knitted-on moss-stitch edging. If you need to join a new ball of yarn while knitting this portion of the front, do so at the side seam where the yarn ends won't be as visible.

◎ To achieve maximum drape, stitches are increased at the center front after the ribbing is completed. The stitches gradually decrease as the front sections narrow, then excess stitches are decreased at the shoulders.

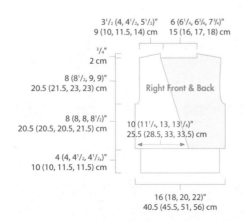

3½ (4, 4½, 5½)"
9 (10, 11.5, 14) cm

6 (6¼, 6¾, 7¾)"
15 (16, 17, 18) cm

¾"
2 cm

8 (8½, 9, 9)"
20.5 (21.5, 23, 23) cm

Right Front & Back

8 (8, 8, 8½)"
20.5 (20.5, 20.5, 21.5) cm

10 (11¼, 13, 13¼)"
25.5 (28.5, 33, 33.5) cm

4 (4, 4½, 4½)"
10 (10, 11.5, 11.5) cm

16 (18, 20, 22)"
40.5 (45.5, 51, 56) cm

Back

With smaller straight needles, CO 96 (108, 120, 132) sts. **Set-up row:** (RS) K1, *k2 through back loops (tbl), p2; rep from * to last 3 sts, k2tbl, k1. **Next row:** (WS) k1, *p2tbl, k2; rep from * to last 3 sts, p2tbl, k1. Maintain twisted rib as established until piece measures 4 (4, 4½, 4½)" (10 [10, 11.5, 11.5] cm) from CO, ending with a WS row. Change to larger needles and cont in St st (knit RS rows; purl WS rows) until piece measures 12 (12, 12½, 13)" (30.5 [30.5, 31.5, 33] cm) from CO, ending with a WS row.

SHAPE ARMHOLES | BO 4 (4, 4, 5) sts at beg of next 2 rows, then BO 3 (4, 5, 6) sts at beg of foll 2 rows, then BO 2 (2, 3, 3) sts at beg of foll 2 rows—78 (88, 96, 104) sts rem. Work even until armholes measure 8 (8½, 9, 9)" (20.5 [21.5, 23, 23] cm), ending with a WS row.

SHAPE SHOULDERS | Mark center 36 (38, 40, 42) sts for neck. BO 6 (7, 6, 9) sts, work to end. **Next row:** (RS) BO 6 (7, 6, 9) sts, work to marked sts, join a second ball of yarn and k36 (38, 40, 42) marked sts, knit to end—15 (18, 22, 22) sts rem. Working each side separately, at each armhole edge BO 6 (7, 6, 9) sts once, then BO rem 9 (11, 16, 13) sts. Place rem 36 (38, 40, 42) sts on holder.

Front

CO and work as for back until piece measures 4 (4, 4½, 4½)" (10 [10, 11.5, 11.5] cm) from CO, ending with a WS row. Break yarn and place first 28 (30, 36, 38) sts on a holder to work later for left side—68 (78, 84, 94) sts rem for right side.

RIGHT SIDE | *Note:* The center front is shaped at the same time as the armhole shaping is introduced; read all the way through the next sections before proceeding. Work 68 (78, 84, 94) right front sts as foll, always working 4 center front sts in moss st: **Inc row:** (RS) Sl 1, p1, k1, p1, k8 (12, 15, 20), [k1f&b, k1] 18 (20, 24, 25) times, knit to end—86 (98, 108, 119) sts. **Next row:** (WS) Sl 1, purl to last 4 sts, [p1, k1] 2 times. **Next row:** (RS) Sl 1, p1, k1, p1, knit to end.

Next row: Sl 1, purl to last 4 sts, [p1, k1] 2 times. Rep the last 2 rows 3 (3, 4, 5) more times, ending with a WS row. Beg with the next row, dec 1 st every 4 rows as foll:

Row 1: (RS) Sl 1, p1, k1, p1, k2, ssk, knit to end—1 st dec'd.

Rows 2 and 4: Sl 1, purl to last 4 sts, [p1, k1] 2 times.

Row 3: Sl 1, p1, k1, p1, knit to end.

Rep these 4 rows 8 (6, 8, 5) more times, then rep Rows 1 and 2 only (i.e., dec 1 st every RS row) 29 (36, 35, 40) times. *At the same time,* when piece measures 12 (12, 12½, 13)" (30.5 [30.5, 31.5, 33] cm) from CO, shape armhole as foll:

Shape Armhole Cont to dec at center front as established, at armhole edge (beg of WS rows), BO 4 (4, 5, 6) sts once, then BO 4 (4, 4, 5) sts once, then BO 2 (2, 3, 3) sts once—38 (45, 52, 59) sts rem when all center front and armhole sts have been dec'd. Cont as established until piece measures 1 row less than back at beg of shoulder shaping, ending with a WS row. **Dec row:** (RS) Sl 1, p1, k1, p1, *k2tog; rep from * to last 0 (1, 0, 3) st(s), k0 (k1, k0, k3tog)—21 (25, 28, 31) sts rem.

Shape Shoulder Keeping in patt as established, at armhole edge (beg of WS rows), BO 6 (7, 6, 9) sts 2 times—9 (11, 16, 13) sts rem. BO all sts in patt.

LEFT SIDE | Place 28 (30, 36, 38) held left front sts onto larger needle. With RS facing, join yarn and work *k1, k1f&b; rep from * to end, then use the backward-loop method (see Glossary) to CO 18 (23, 24, 23) sts—60 (68, 78, 80) sts total. **Next row:** (WS) Sl 1, p1, k1, p1, purl to end. **Next row:** (RS) Knit to last 4 sts, [p1, k1] 2 times. Rep the last 2 rows until piece measures 12 (12, 12½, 13)" (30.5 [30.5, 31.5, 33] cm) from CO, ending with a WS row. Keeping the 4 center front edge sts in moss st as established, cont as foll:

Shape Armhole and Neck **Next row:** (RS) Keeping in patt as established, BO 4 (4, 4, 5) sts, knit to last 8 sts, k2tog, k2, work 4 edge sts. Work 1 (WS) row even in patt. **Next row:** (RS) BO 4 (4, 5, 6) sts, knit to last 8 sts, k2tog, k2, work 4 edge sts. Work 1 (WS) row even sts in patt. **Next row:** (RS) BO 2 (2, 3, 3) sts, knit to last 8 sts, k2tog, k2, work 4 edge sts. Work 1 (WS) row even in patt. Keeping in patt, dec 1 st at front neck edge in this manner every RS row 9 (13, 17, 13) more times—38 (42, 46, 50) sts rem. Cont even until piece measures 1 row less than back at beg of shoulder shaping, ending with a RS row. **Dec row:** (RS) *K2tog; rep from * to last 4 (8, 10, 12) sts, k0 (4, 6, 8), work rem 4 sts as established—21 (25, 28, 32) sts rem.

Shape Shoulder Keeping in patt as established, at armhole edge (beg of RS rows), BO 6 (7, 6, 9) sts 2 times—9 (11, 16, 13) sts rem. BO all sts in patt.

Finishing

Gently steam-block pieces, being careful not to stretch the stitches. With yarn threaded on a tapestry needle, sew front to back at shoulders. Sew side seams. Carefully tack down CO edge of lower left front to WS, just above ribbing. Weave in loose ends.

ARMBANDS | With smaller cir needle and RS facing, pick up and knit 84 (90, 96, 96) sts evenly spaced around armhole. Place marker (pm) and join for working in rnds. Work in moss st (see Stitch Guide) for 4 rnds. BO all sts in patt.

BACK NECK EDGING | Transfer 36 (38, 40, 42) held back neck sts onto smaller needle. Work 4 rows in moss st. BO all sts in patt. Carefully sew each edge of back neck edging to front neck.

Cowlneck Pullover

LAURA GRUTZECK

Paired yarnovers shape the cowl and sleeves while giving a feminine look to this sleek and simple pullover. The pieces are trimmed with narrow, non-binding garter-stitch bands. Worked in a drapey alpaca yarn, this sweater is luxuriously soft and warm without a bit of bulk.

Finished Size 36 (40, 44, 48)" (91.5 [101.5, 112, 128] cm) bust circumference. Sweater shown measures 36" (91.5 cm).

Yarn Fingering weight (#1 Fine). *Shown here:* Garnstudio Drops Alpaca (100% alpaca; 180 m/ 100 g): #3720 rose, 7 (8, 9, 12) balls.

Needles U.S. size 3 (3.25 mm): 24" (60 cm) circular. Adjust needle size if necessary to obtain the correct gauge.

Notions Markers (m); stitch holders; tapestry needle.

Gauge 26 stitches and 34 rows = 4" (10 cm) in stockinette stitch.

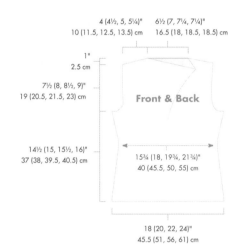

4 (4½, 5, 5¼)"
10 (11.5, 12.5, 13.5) cm

6½ (7, 7¼, 7¼)"
16.5 (18, 18.5, 18.5) cm

1"
2.5 cm

7½ (8, 8½, 9)"
19 (20.5, 21.5, 23) cm

Front & Back

14½ (15, 15½, 16)"
37 (38, 39.5, 40.5) cm

15¾ (18, 19¾, 21¾)"
40 (45.5, 50, 55) cm

18 (20, 22, 24)"
45.5 (51, 56, 61) cm

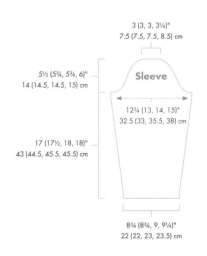

3 (3, 3, 3¼)"
7.5 (7.5, 7.5, 8.5) cm

5½ (5¾, 5¾, 6)"
14 (14.5, 14.5, 15) cm

Sleeve

12¾ (13, 14, 15)"
32.5 (33, 35.5, 38) cm

17 (17½, 18, 18)"
43 (44.5, 45.5, 45.5) cm

8¾ (8¾, 9, 9¼)"
22 (22, 23, 23.5) cm

Notes

◎ Knit the first and last stitch of every row for selvedge sts. Selvedge stitches are not included in the finished circumference.

◎ When working the front, you will be working increases on every RS row for the cowl. If your row gauge is different than that stated, you will end up working more or fewer increases when your piece measures the desired length. This is not a problem. When you place markers for the neck set up, just make sure you have the required number of sts on each side of the markers for shoulders. Any missing or additional sts will fall in the center, between the markers, to make a smaller or larger cowl. Follow the rest of the directions for the front shaping, the only change will be in the number of sts you bind off for the cowl.

Back

CO 119 (133, 145, 157) sts. Work garter st (knit every row) until piece measures 1" (2.5 cm) from CO. Knitting the first and last st of every row, work center 117 (131, 143, 155) sts in St st (knit RS rows; purl WS rows) until piece measures 2½ (3, 3½, 4)" (6.5 [7.5, 9, 10] cm) from CO, ending with a RS row. **Next row:** (WS) Place markers (pm) as foll: K1 (selvedge st), p43 (48, 52, 56), pm, p31 (35, 39, 43), pm, purl to last st, k1 (selvedge st). **Dec row:** (RS) K1, ssk, knit to 2 sts before m, ssk, slip marker (sl m), knit to next marker, sl m, k2tog, knit to last 3 sts, k2tog, k1—4 sts dec'd. Work 7 rows even. Rep the last 8 rows 3 more times—103 (117, 129, 141) sts rem. Cont even until piece measures 6½ (7½, 8½, 9)" (16.5 [19, 21.5, 23] cm) from CO, ending with a WS row. **Inc row:** (RS) K1, M1R (see Glossary), knit to marker, M1R, sl m, knit to next marker, sl m, M1L (see Glossary), knit to last stitch, M1L, k1—4 sts inc'd. Work 7 rows even. Rep the last 8 rows 3 more times—119 (133, 145, 157) sts. Remove markers. Cont even until piece measures 14½ (15, 15½, 16)" (37 [38, 39.5, 40.5] cm) from CO, ending with a WS row.

SHAPE ARMHOLES | BO 7 (7, 8, 9) sts at beg of next 2 rows—105 (119, 129, 139) sts rem. Dec 1 st each end of needle every RS row 5 (7, 9, 12) times as foll: K1, ssk, knit to last 3 sts, k2tog, k1—95 (105, 111, 115) sts rem when all decs have been completed. Work even until armholes measure 7½ (8, 8½, 9)" (19 [20.5, 21.5, 23] cm) from CO, ending with a WS row.

SHAPE SHOULDERS | BO 7 (8, 8, 9) sts at beg of next 4 rows, then BO 6 (7, 8, 8) sts at beg of foll 4 rows—43 (45, 47, 47) sts rem. Place sts on holder.

Front

Note: Center front increases occur at the same time as armhole shaping is introduced; read all the way through the foll sections before proceeding. CO and work as for back until piece measures 11 (12, 13, 13½)" (28 [30.5, 33, 34.5] cm) from CO, ending with a WS row. Mark the center 60th (67th, 73rd, 79th) st. **Inc row:** (RS) Knit to marked center st, yo, k1 (center st), yo, knit to end—2 sts inc'd. Work 1 WS row even. Rep these 2 rows 14 (12, 10, 10) more times—149 (159, 167, 179) sts. Piece should measure about 14½ (15, 15½, 16)" (37 [38, 39.5, 40.5] cm) from CO.

SHAPE ARMHOLES Cont working center front incs, BO 7 (7, 8, 9) sts at beg of next 2 rows, then dec 1 st each end of needle every RS row 5 (7, 9, 12) times—137 (147, 153, 163) sts. Work even until armhole measures 7½ (8, 8½, 9)" (19 [20.5, 21.5, 23] cm), ending with a WS row—189 (199, 205, 213) sts when all incs and decs have been completed (see Notes). Remove center marker.

SHAPE NECK (RS) K26 (30, 32, 34), pm, k137 (139, 141, 145), pm, knit to end—26 (30, 32, 34) sts rem each side for shoulders; 137 (139, 141, 145) center sts.

SHAPE SHOULDERS Working the center sts in garter st and the shoulder sts in St st, BO 7 (8, 8, 9) sts at beg of next 4 rows, then BO 6 (7, 8, 8) sts at beg of foll 4 rows. **Next row:** K9 and place these sts on holder, BO next 119 (121, 123, 127) sts for cowl, k9 and place these 9 sts on another holder.

Sleeves (make 2)

CO 57 (57, 59, 61) sts. Work in garter st until piece measures 1" (2.5 cm) from CO. Knitting the first and last st every row, work center 55 (55, 57, 59) sts in St st until piece measures 1½" (3.8 cm) from CO, ending with a RS row. **Next row:** (WS) K1, p27 (27, 28, 29), mark next st, purl to last st, k1. **Inc row:** (RS) Knit to marked st, yo, k1 (marked st), yo, knit to end—2 sts inc'd. Work 5 rows even. Rep the last 6 rows 12 (13, 15, 17) more times—83 (85, 91, 97) sts. Work even in St st until piece measures 17 (17½, 18, 18)" (43 [44.5, 45.5, 45.5] cm) from CO, ending with a WS row.

SHAPE CAP BO 7 (7, 8, 9) sts at beg of next 2 rows—69 (71, 75, 79) sts rem. **Next row:** (RS) K1, ssk, knit to last 3 sts, k2tog, k1—2 sts dec'd. Work 1 WS row even. Rep the last 2 rows 19 (20, 18, 20) more times—29 (29, 37, 37) sts rem. **Next row:** (WS) K1, p2tog, purl to last 3 sts, p2tog through back loops (tbl), k1—2 sts dec'd. Cont to dec 1 st each end of needle every row (foll instructions for RS row dec on RS and WS row decs on WS rows) 4 (4, 8, 7) more times—19 (19, 19, 21) sts rem. BO all sts.

Finishing

Block pieces to measurements. With yarn threaded on a tapestry needle, sew front to back at shoulders. Place 9 held sts from viewer's left side of front on cir needle. Place held back sts on the same needle—the 9 sts from the front will be on the right side of the needle, the back sts will be on the left. Beg with the 9 sts on the left, work a garter st edging BO as foll: *K8, k2tog (1 st from 9 front sts plus 1 st from back), turn work, k9; rep from * until no back sts rem. With yarn threaded on a tapestry needle, use the Kitchener st (see Glosssary) to graft the 9 sts on needle to the 9 held sts of right front.

Weave in loose ends. Sew sleeve caps into armholes. Sew sleeve and side seams. Block again if desired.

Cabled Vest

LISA R. MYERS

Slouchy and comfortable, this vest has an easy fit that's a little "retro" without being totally "Flashdance." To keep the traditional look without a blousy effect, the ribbing is worked on the same size needle with more stitches than the body. To simplify the knitting, this vest is worked inside out so that most of the stitches are knitted (which most knitters prefer) rather than purled (which most knitters don't).

Finished Size 32 (36, 40, 44, 48)" (81.5 [91.5, 101.5, 112, 122] cm) bust circumference. Vest shown measures 40" (101.5 cm).

Yarn Fingering weight (#1 Super Fine). *Shown here:* Filatura di Crosa Zarina (100% merino; 181 yd [165 m]/50 g): #1396 cream, 5 (6, 6, 7, 8) balls.

Needles U.S. size 4 (3.5 mm): 16" and 24" (40 and 60 cm) circular. Adjust needle size if necessary to obtain the correct gauge.

Notions Markers (m); cable needle (cn); tapestry needle.

Gauge 26 stitches and 34 rows = 4" (10 cm) in stockinette stitch.

Notes

◎ Instructions are given for working this vest inside out to facilitate the cable pattern.
◎ The body is worked in a single piece in the round to the armholes, then the front and back are worked separately in rows to the shoulders.

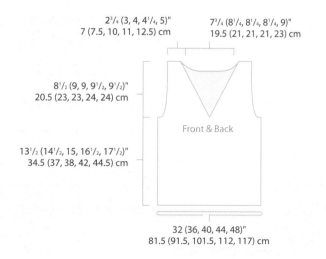

2³⁄₄ (3, 4, 4¹⁄₄, 5)"
7 (7.5, 10, 11, 12.5) cm

7³⁄₄ (8¹⁄₄, 8¹⁄₄, 8¹⁄₄, 9)"
19.5 (21, 21, 21, 23) cm

8¹⁄₂ (9, 9, 9¹⁄₂, 9¹⁄₂)"
20.5 (23, 23, 24, 24) cm

Front & Back

13¹⁄₂ (14¹⁄₂, 15, 16¹⁄₂, 17¹⁄₂)"
34.5 (37, 38, 42, 44.5) cm

32 (36, 40, 44, 48)"
81.5 (91.5, 101.5, 112, 117) cm

Body

With longer cir needle, CO 260 (292, 324, 356, 388) sts. Place marker (pm) and join for working in rnds, being careful not to twist sts. Work in k1, p1 rib until piece measures 2¼ (2½, 2½, 2¾, 3)" (5.5 [6.5, 6.5, 7, 7.5] cm) from CO. **Dec rnd:** K2; *k3, k2tog, k3, k2tog, k4, k2tog; rep from * to last 2 sts, k2—212 (238, 264, 290, 316) sts rem. **Set up cable panel:** K15 (18, 21, 27, 30), pm, work Rnd 1 of Cable Panel chart over next 12 sts, pm, k158 (177, 197, 211, 232), pm, work Rnd 11 (so that cables will mirror at shoulder) of cable patt over next 12 sts, pm, k15 (19, 22, 28, 30). Work in patt as established until piece measures 13½ (14½, 15, 16½, 17½)" (34.5 [37, 38, 42, 44.5] cm) from CO edge, ending 6 (7, 7, 9, 9) sts before end of rnd m on an even-numbered rnd.

DIVIDE FOR FRONT AND BACK | BO 12 (13, 13, 17, 18) sts, work in patt until there are 94 (106, 119, 128, 140) sts on right needle, turn work around. From this point onward, vest is worked back and forth in rows. Odd-numbered rows of cable patt are unchanged; on even-numbered (WS) rows, sts are worked as they appear (knit the knits; purl the purls).

FRONT | *Note:* The armholes and neck are shaped at the same time; read all the way through the next sections before proceeding. Working 94 (106, 119, 128, 140) front sts in patt as established, beg with the next row, dec 1 st each end of needle every RS row 5 (7, 7, 10, 10) times ending with a WS row and *at the same time,* after 2 sets of decs are complete, divide for neck.

Divide for Neck Next row: (RS) Work 44 (50, 57, 61, 67) sts, k2tog, join a second ball of yarn, k2tog, work rem 46 (52, 58, 63, 69) sts—47 (53, 59, 64, 70) sts rem for right shoulder, 45 (51, 58, 62, 68) sts rem for left shoulder. *Note:* The side with the cable has 1 or 2 more sts than the other side to compensate for draw-in. Working each side separately, cont working armhole decs and *at the same time* dec 1 st at each neck edge every 3rd row 24 (26, 26, 26, 28) times—18 (20, 26, 28, 32) sts rem for right shoulder and 16 (18, 25, 26, 30) sts rem for left shoulder when all neck and armhole decs have been completed. Cont even until armhole measures 8½ (9, 9, 9½, 9½)" (21.5 [23, 23, 24, 24] cm), ending with a WS row. BO all sts, working 4 cable sts as [p2tog] 2 times.

BACK | With knit side facing, rejoin yarn to 106 (119, 132, 145, 158) held sts. BO 12 (13, 13, 17, 18) sts, work in patt to end. Dec 1 st each end of needle every other row 5 (7, 7, 10, 10) times—84 (92, 105, 108, 120) sts rem. Cont even until armholes measure same length as front to shoulder, making sure to end with same row of cable panel. BO all sts, working 4 cable sts as [p2tog] 2 times.

Finishing

With yarn threaded on a tapestry needle, sew front to back at shoulders so that the stockinette side is the RS. Sew side seams.

NECKBAND | With shorter cir needle, RS facing, and beg at right shoulder, pick up and knit 48 (52, 52, 52, 56) sts along back neck, 66 (72, 72, 72, 78) sts along left front neck, 1 st at center front, and 66 (72, 72, 72, 78) sts along right front neck—181 (197, 197, 197, 213) sts total. Mark center front st. Join for working in rnds. Work in k1, p1 rib, and *at the same time* dec at center front as foll: Work rib to 1 st before marked st, sl 2 sts tog kwise, k1, p2sso, cont in rib with same st that preceded dec. Rep this rnd 5 more times, ending 1 st before end of rnd. BO all sts, working k2tog for every BO st.

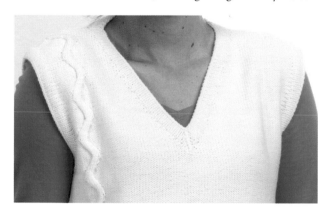

ARMHOLE EDGING | With shorter cir needle, RS facing, and beg at center of underarm, pick up and knit about 166 (180, 180, 190, 190) sts evenly spaced around armhole. Join for working in rnds. Work k1, p1 rib for 5 rnds. BO all sts, working k2tog as for neckband.

Weave in loose ends. Block to measurements.

CABLE PANEL

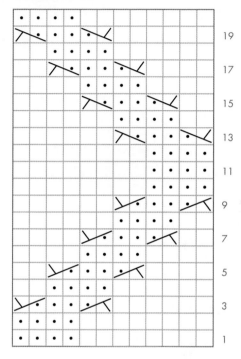

 k on RS; p on WS

 p on RS; k on WS

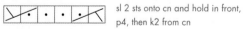 sl 2 sts onto cn and hold in front, p4, then k2 from cn

 sl 4 sts onto cn, hold in back, k2, then p4 from cn

*Note: Vest is worked inside out.

Kimono Top

LISA R. MYERS

This loose-fitting top is based on typical kimono construction—simple rectangles for the back and sleeves and modified rectangles for the fronts. Even the bamboo yarn has Asian roots. The butterflies in the stitch pattern are simply floats worked on top of one another, then gathered up into a single stitch. For a night out or lounging around the boudoir, this supple and lustrous wrap can be sexy or elegant—or both!

Finished Size 29 (32, 36, 39, 42, 46, 49)" (73.5 [81.5, 91.5, 99, 106.5, 117, 124.5] cm) bust circumference, fastened. Kimono shown measures 36" (91.5 cm).

Yarn Sportweight (#2 Fine).
Shown here: Rowan Classic Yarn Bamboo Soft (100% bamboo; 112 yd [102 m]/50 g): #110 pompadour, 12 (14, 15, 16, 18, 18, 20) balls.

Needles U.S. size 4 (3.5 mm). Adjust needle size if necessary to obtain the correct gauge.

Notions Markers (m); stitch holders; tapestry needle.

Gauge 24 stitches and 48 rows = 4" (10 cm) in little butterfly stitch pattern.

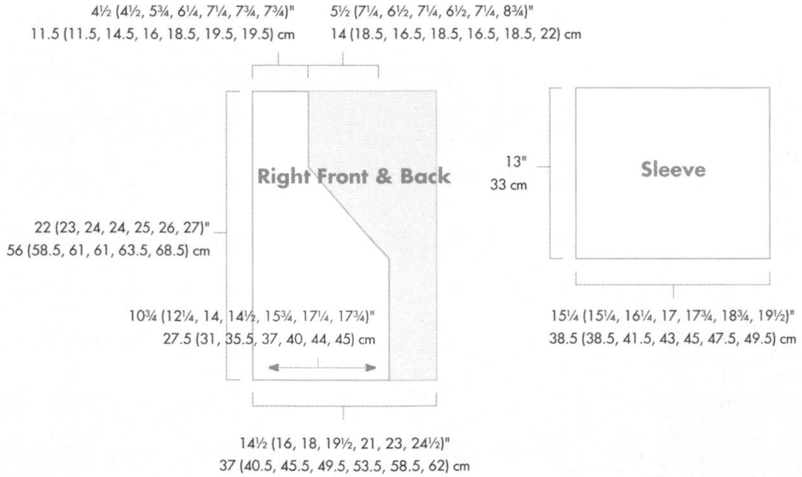

Stitch Guide

Little Butterfly Stitch
(multiple of 10 sts + 7)

Rows 1, 3, and 5: (RS) K1, *k5, sl 5 with yarn in front (wyf); rep from * to last 6 sts, k6.

Rows 2 and 4: Purl.

Row 6: P8, *use right-hand needle to draw loop up purlwise under the floats, p1, pass the gathering loop over the purled st, p9; rep from * to last 9 sts, use right-hand needle to draw loop up purlwise under the floats, p1, pass the gathering loop over the purled st, p8.

Rows 7, 9, and 11: K1, *sl 5 wyf, k5; rep from * to last 6 sts, sl 5, k1.

Rows 8 and 10: Purl.

Row 12: P3, *use right-hand needle to draw loop up purlwise under the floats, p1, pass the gathering loop over the purled st, p9; rep from * to last 4 sts, use right-hand needle to draw loop up purlwise under the floats, p1, pass the gathering loop over the purled st, p3.

Repeat Rows 1–12 for pattern.

4½ (4½, 5¾, 6¼, 7¼, 7¾, 7¾)"
11.5 (11.5, 14.5, 16, 18.5, 19.5, 19.5) cm

5½ (7¼, 6½, 7¼, 6½, 7¼, 8¾)"
14 (18.5, 16.5, 18.5, 16.5, 18.5, 22) cm

Right Front & Back

22 (23, 24, 24, 25, 26, 27)"
56 (58.5, 61, 61, 63.5, 68.5) cm

10¾ (12¼, 14, 14½, 15¾, 17¼, 17¾)"
27.5 (31, 35.5, 37, 40, 44, 45) cm

14½ (16, 18, 19½, 21, 23, 24½)"
37 (40.5, 45.5, 49.5, 53.5, 58.5, 62) cm

13"
33 cm

Sleeve

15¼ (15¼, 16¼, 17, 17¾, 18¾, 19½)"
38.5 (38.5, 41.5, 43, 45, 47.5, 49.5) cm

Note

◎ Because this garment has a drop shoulder and because there's no correlation between bust circumference and shoulder width, sleeve length is highly individual. To calculate yours, hold your arm slightly bent and measure from your spine at the back of your neck to a point midway between your elbow and your wrist. Subtract one-quarter of the finished bust circumference of the kimono (or one-half the back width) from this length to determine your optimum sleeve length.

◎ As decreases are worked on the fronts, there will not always be an even multiple of the pattern repeat. Work the partial pattern repeats in stockinette stitch.

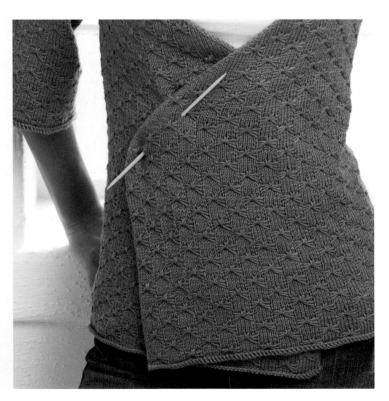

Back

CO 87 (97, 107, 117, 127, 137, 147) sts. Purl 1 row, knit 1 row, then purl 1 row. Work Rows 1–12 of little butterfly st (see Stitch Guide) until piece measures 22 (23, 24, 24, 25, 26, 27)" (56 [58.5, 61, 61, 63.5, 68.5] cm) from CO. Place sts on holder.

Right Front

CO 64 (74, 84, 87, 94, 104, 107) sts. Purl 1 row, knit 1 row, then purl 1 row. **Next row:** (RS) Sl 2 with yarn in back (wyb), *k5, sl 5 with yarn in front (wyf); rep from * to last 11 (11, 11, 6, 11, 11, 6) sts, sl 5 (5, 5, 0, 5, 5, 0) with yarn in front (wyf), k1 (1, 1, 6, 1, 1, 6). Cont in patt as established, slipping the first 2 sts of every RS row for I-cord edge, until piece measures 8 (8½, 9, 9, 10, 11, 12)" (20.5 [21.5, 23, 23, 25.5, 28, 30.5] cm) from CO, ending with a WS row.

SHAPE FRONT EDGE | **Dec row:** (RS) Sl 2 wyb, ssk, work in patt to end of row—1 st dec'd. Dec 1 st at front edge in this manner every 2 (2, 2, 2, 2, 2 of 3, 2 of 3) rows 36 (46, 49, 49, 49, 56, 59) more times (*Note:* To dec on WS rows, purl to last 4 sts, p2togtbl, p2)—27 (27, 34, 37, 44, 47, 47) sts rem. Cont even in patt until piece measures same as back. Place sts on holder.

Left Front

CO 64 (74, 84, 87, 94, 104, 107) sts. Purl 1 row, knit 1 row, then purl 1 row. **Next row:** (RS) *k5, sl 5 with yarn in front (wyf); rep from * to last 8 (8, 8, 3, 8, 8, 3) sts, sl 5 (5, 5, 0, 5, 5, 0) with yarn in front (wyf), k3. **Next row:** Sl 2 wyf, purl to end. Cont in patt as established until piece measures 8 (8½, 9, 9, 10, 11, 12)" (20.5 [21.5, 23, 23, 25.5, 28, 30.5] cm) from CO, ending with a WS row.

SHAPE FRONT EDGE | **Dec row:** (RS) Work in patt to last 4 sts, k2tog, k2—1 st dec'd. Dec 1 st at front edge in this manner every 2 (2, 2, 2, 2, 2 of 3, 2 of 3) rows 36 (46, 49, 49, 49, 56, 59) more times (*Note:* To dec on WS rows, sl 2 wyf, p2tog, purl to end)—27 (27, 34, 37, 44, 47, 47) sts rem. Cont even in patt until piece measures same as back. Place sts on holder.

Sleeves (make 2)

CO 92, (92, 97, 102, 107, 112, 117) sts. Purl 1 row, knit 1 row, then purl 1 row. Beg with Row 1, work little butterfly st until piece measures 13" (33 cm) or desired length to armhole, ending with Row 6 or 12 of patt. BO all sts knitwise.

Finishing

JOIN SHOULDERS | Place 87 (97, 107, 117, 127, 137, 147) held left back sts on one needle, then place 27 (27, 34, 37, 44, 47, 47) held left front sts on a dpn. With WS facing tog, hold the two needles parallel to each other and work I-cord BO as foll: CO 3 sts and place on front needle. With a third needle, *k2, sl 1 knitwise, sl first st on front left-hand needle knitwise, sl first st on back left-hand needle knitwise, insert tip of either left-hand needle into all 3 slipped sts from back to front and k3tog, sl 3 sts from right-hand needle onto front left-hand needle purlwise, and pull yarn across back of sts; rep from * until all front sts have been worked. Cont to work I-cord BO across back neck sts, working k2tog instead of k3tog to join I-cord band to neck, until 27 (27, 34, 37, 44, 47, 47) sts rem for other shoulder. Place held sts from right front on dpn, hold parallel to needle with back sts, and complete I-cord BO across second shoulder as for first shoulder.

SEAMS | Place markers 7½ (7½, 8, 8½, 9, 9½, 10)" (19 [19, 20.5, 21.5, 23, 24, 25.5] cm) down from shoulder seam on fronts and back. Match center of sleeve top to shoulder seam and with yarn threaded on a tapestry needle, sew sleeve to front and back between markers. Sew side and sleeve seams. Weave in loose ends. Block lightly.

Speed

We won't lie to you: A sweater (or any other project for that matter) knitted at a gauge of 7 or 8 stitches to the inch will take longer than one knitted at 3 or 4 stitches to the inch. But we think the benefits are well worth the extra time, and we think you will, too. If you're challenged for time or have a short attention span, this chapter is for you. All of the following projects were designed with speed in mind—from smaller projects to creative techniques such as doubling the yarn or using larger needles to create looser gauges.

Projects

Ribby Vest

Anemone Beret

Eyelet Halter

Mohair T-Neck

Dolman Top

Ribby Vest

CAROL SULCOSKI

This sexy, close-fitting vest takes advantage of the melange color effects of Trekking sock yarn. Two strands held together speed the knitting while creating color gradations that resemble an impressionistic painting. The color pattern in the stripes on the front follows a formula; the back is worked in random colors. This piece is great for layering—it goes with almost every color. Make a pair of matching socks out of the leftover yarn!

Finished Size 32 (36, 40, 44)" (81.5 [91.5, 101.5, 112] cm) bust circumference, slightly stretched. Sweater shown measures 36" (91.5 cm). To fit 30–32 (34–36, 38–40, 42–44)" (76–81.5 [86.5–91.5, 96.5–101.5, 106.5–112] cm) bust. *Note:* The ribbed pattern has a lot of stretch and will accommodate a range of sizes.

Yarn Fingering weight (#1 Super Fine). *Shown here:* Zitron Trekking XXL (75% wool, 25% nylon; 462 yd [422 m/100 g]: #110 coral/pink mix (A), #107 green/coral mix (B), and #108 blue/turquoise/green mix (E), 1 skein each (all sizes); #91 (C) deep rose mix and #104 blue mix (D), 1 (1, 1, 2, 2) skeins each.

Needles Body—U. S. size 5 (3.75 mm). Edging—U.S. size 4 (3.5 mm): 16" (40 cm) circular (cir). Adjust needle size if necessary to obtain the correct gauge.

Notions Markers (m); stitch holders; safety pin or small stitch holder; tapestry needle.

Gauge 24 stitches and 32 rows = 4" (10 cm) in k2, p2 ribbing on larger needles with 2 strands of yarn held together, slightly stretched.

Stitch Guide
Muted Stripe Pattern
Holding 1 strand of each color tog, work 14 rows each of the foll combinations:
A and B
C and E
A and D
B and C
E and A
D and B
C and A
D and E

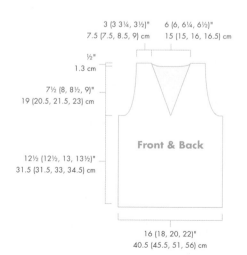

3 (3 3¼, 3½)"
7.5 (7.5, 8.5, 9) cm

6 (6, 6¼, 6½)"
15 (15, 16, 16.5) cm

½"
1.3 cm

7½ (8, 8½, 9)"
19 (20.5, 21.5, 23) cm

12½ (12½, 13, 13½)"
31.5 (31.5, 33, 34.5) cm

Front & Back

16 (18, 20, 22)"
40.5 (45.5, 51, 56) cm

Notes

◎ Two strands of yarn are worked together throughout; the combination of colors in the two strands varies to form the muted stripe pattern.

◎ Knit the first and last stitch of every row for selvedge stitches.

◎ Knit the front first to ensure you have enough yarn to work the stripe pattern; the back is worked in random stripes that can be altered if necessary to accommodate the remaining yarn.

◎ Work all decreases one stitch in from the edge on right-side rows as follows: K1, ssk at the beg of rows; k2tog, k1 at the end of rows.

◎ The rib pattern for the front and back are slightly different.

Front

With 2 strands of C held tog and smaller cir needle, CO 94 (110, 118, 134) sts. Do not join. Working back and forth in rows, change to 2 strands of D and work rib patt as foll:

Row 1: (RS) K3, [p2, k2] 8 (10, 11, 13) times to center 24 sts, place marker (pm), p2, k4, p2, k8, p2, k4, p2, pm, [k2, p2] 8 (10, 11, 13) times to last 3 sts, k3.

Row 2: (WS) K1, work sts as they appear (knit the knits and purl the purls) to last st, k1.

Rep Rows 1 and 2 until piece measures 1½" (3.8 cm) from CO, ending with a WS row. Change to larger needles and muted stripe patt (see Stitch Guide), working 14 rows of each color combination and maintaining rib patt as established until piece measures 12½ (12½, 13, 13½)" (31.5 [31.5, 33, 34.5] cm) from CO, ending with a WS row.

SHAPE ARMHOLES AND NECK | *Note:* The armholes and neck are shaped at the same time; read all the way through the foll section before proceeding. When binding off sts, do so in pattern. With RS facing and keeping in patt, BO 4 (5, 6, 7) sts, work to end. **Next row:** (WS) BO 4 (5, 6, 7) sts, work to center 2 sts (center 2 sts of k8 in middle rib section), place these 2 sts on holder, join a second ball of yarn and work to end—42 (49, 52, 59) sts rem each side. Working each side separately and keeping in rib and color patts as established, at each armhole edge BO 2 (2, 2, 3) sts once. Cont in patt, dec 1 st at each armhole edge every RS row 7 (10, 10, 11) times and *at the same time*, at each neck edge BO 2 sts 3 (4, 4, 4) times then dec 1 st every RS row 4 (6, 6, 7) times—18 (18, 20, 22) sts rem each side after all armhole and neck shaping is complete. Cont even in patt until armholes measure 7½" (8, 8½, 9)" (19 [20.5, 21.5, 23] cm), ending with a WS row.

SHAPE SHOULDERS | At each armhole edge BO 6 (6, 7, 8) sts 2 times. BO rem 6 sts.

Back

With 2 strands of C held tog and smaller cir needle, CO 100 (108, 120, 132) sts. Do not join. Working back and forth in rows, change to 2 strands of D and work rib patt as foll:

Row 1: (RS) K1, [p2, k2] 7 (8, 9, 10) times, p2, k8, p2, [k2, p2] 5 (5, 6, 7) times, k8, [p2, k2] 7 (8, 9, 10) times, p2, k1.

Row 2: (WS) K1, work sts as they appear (knit the knits and purl the purls) to last st, k1.

Work as for front until piece measures 1½" (3.8 cm) from CO, ending with a WS row. Change to larger needles and work with 2 strands of different-colored yarns, changing 1 strand at a time randomly and maintaining rib patt as established until piece measures 12½ (12½, 13, 13½)" (31.5 [31.5, 33, 34.5] cm) from CO, ending with a WS row.

SHAPE ARMHOLES | BO 4 (5, 6, 7) sts at beg of next 2 rows, then BO 3 (3, 4, 5) sts at beg of foll 2 rows—86 (92, 100, 108) rem. Dec 1 st each end of needle every RS row 7 (10, 11, 12) times—72 (72, 78, 84) sts rem. Cont even in patt until armholes measure 7½ (8, 8½, 9)" (19 [20.5, 21.5, 23] cm), ending with a WS row.

SHAPE SHOULDERS | Mark center 36 (36, 38, 40) sts for neck. **Next row:** (RS) BO 6 (6, 7, 8) sts, work to end. **Next row:** (WS) BO 6 (6, 7, 8) sts, place marked 36 (36, 38, 40) sts on a holder, join a second ball of yarn and knit to end—12 (12, 13, 14) sts rem each side. Working each side separately, at each armhole edge BO 6 (6, 7, 8) sts once, then BO rem 6 sts.

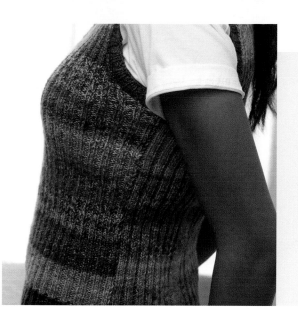

Finishing

Weave in loose ends. Gently steam-block pieces, being careful not to stretch out or flatten ribbing. With yarn threaded on a tapestry needle, sew front to back at shoulders. Sew side seams.

ARMBANDS | With 2 strands of D held tog, smaller cir needle, and RS facing, pick up and knit 96 (100, 108, 112) sts evenly spaced around armhole. Pm and join for working in rnds. Work in k2, p2 rib until band measures 1" (2.5 cm) from pick-up rnd. BO all sts in patt.

NECKBAND | With 2 stands of C held tog, smaller cir needle, RS facing, and beg at left shoulder seam, pick up and knit 53 (53, 57, 70) sts along left front, pm, k2 held center front sts, pm, pick up and knit 53 (53, 57, 70) sts along right front, then k36 (36, 38, 40) held back neck sts—144 (144, 154, 182) sts total. Pm and join for working in rnds.

Rnd 1: Work in k2, p2 rib to 2 sts before marked center sts, ssk, k2, k2tog, cont in k2, p2 rib to end of rnd.

Rep this rnd until band measures 1" (2.5 cm) from pick-up rnd, maintaining rib patt on each side of marked center sts. BO all sts in patt.

Finished Size 18" (45.7 cm)
brim circumference, unstretched.
To fit an average woman's head.

Yarn Fingering weight
(#1 Super Fine).
Shown here: Koigu Premium Merino
(100% merino; 175 yd
[160 m]/50 g): #2174 blue, 2 skeins.

Needles Body—U.S. size 4
(3.5 mm): 16" (40 cm) circular (cir)
and set of 4 or 5 double-pointed (dpn).
Ribbing—U.S. size 2 (3 mm):
16" (40 cm) cir. Adjust needle
size if necessary to obtain the
correct gauge.

Notions Marker (m);
tapestry needle.

Gauge 28 stitches and
36 rows = 4" (10 cm)
in stockinette stitch worked in the
round on larger needle.

Anemone Beret

CAROL SULCOSKI

A lightweight hat is much less likely to plaster your hair to your scalp, resulting in the dreaded hat-hair, than a dense, heavy hat. This cheeky beret, knitted in a luscious handdyed merino, will keep you toasty warm while looking great. The textured stitch pattern illustrates how fine-gauge yarns can go where bulkier ones can't: The detail of this stitch pattern would be lost in a thick yarn, and you'd have a lumpy mess instead of a pleasing pebbled texture.

Beret

With smaller needle, CO 128 sts. Place marker (pm) and join for working in rnds, being careful not to twist sts. Work in k2, p2 rib until piece measures 1½" (3.8 cm) from CO. Change to larger cir needle and inc as foll: *K2, M1 (see Glossary); rep from *—192 sts. Rep Rnds 1–4 of anemone st (see Stitch Guide) until piece measures about 5" (12.5 cm) from inc rnd, ending with Rnd 4 of patt. **Dec Rnd 1**: (Rnd 1 of patt), *k2tog wrapping yarn twice around needle, k2 wrapping yarn twice; rep from * —144 sts rem. Work Rnds 2–4 of patt, then work Rnds 1 (without decreases) and 2 once more. **Dec Rnd 2**: (Rnd 3 of patt) K2, *k1 wrapping yarn twice, k2tog wrapping yarn twice, k1 wrapping yarn twice; rep from * to last 2 sts, k2tog—108 sts rem. Work Rnd 4 of patt, then work Rnds 1–4 once more. **Dec Rnd 3**: (Rnd 1 of patt) K1 wrapping yarn twice, *k2tog wrapping yarn twice, k2 wrapping yarn twice; rep from * to last 7 sts, [k2tog wrapping yarn twice] 3 times, k1 wrapping yarn twice—80 sts

rem. *Note:* Change to dpn when there are too few sts to fit comfortably on cir needle. Work Rnds 2–4 of patt. **Dec Rnd 4**: (Rnd 1 of patt) K1 wrapping yarn twice, *k2tog wrapping yarn twice, k2 wrapping yarn twice; rep from * to last 7 sts, [k2tog wrapping yarn twice] 2 times, k3 wrapping yarn twice—60 sts rem. Work Rnd 2 of patt. **Dec Rnd 5**: (Rnd 3 of patt) K2, *k1 wrapping yarn twice, k2tog wrapping yarn twice, k1 wrapping yarn twice; rep from * to last 6 sts, k2tog wrapping yarn twice, [k2tog] 2 times—44 sts rem. Work Rnd 4 of patt. **Dec Rnd 6**: (Rnd 1 of patt) K2 wrapping yarn twice, *k2tog wrapping yarn twice; rep from * to last 2 sts, k2 wrapping yarn twice—24 sts rem. Work Rnd 2 of patt.

Finishing

Break yarn, thread tail on a tapestry needle, and draw through rem sts. Fasten off to the WS. Weave in loose ends. Block lightly.

Stitch Guide

**Anemone Stitch
(multiple of 4 sts)**

Rnd 1: *K1 wrapping yarn twice around needle; rep from *.

Rnd 2: *Sl 4 sts individually while dropping extra loops, return these sts to left needle, [knit these 4 sts tog, but do not drop the sts from the left needle, purl the same 4 sts tog but do not drop the sts from the left needle] 2 times, drop the original 4 sts from the left needle; rep from * to end of rnd.

Rnd 3: K2, *k1 wrapping yarn twice around needle; rep from * to last 2 sts, k2.

Rnd 4: K2, *sl 4 sts individually while dropping extra loops, return these sts to left needle, [knit these 4 sts tog, then purl these 4 sts tog] 2 times as in Rnd 2; rep from * to last 2 sts, k2.

Repeat Rounds 1–4 for pattern.

Eyelet Halter

LAURA GRUTZECK

Worked in the round and trimmed with a simple band of I-cord, this little halter knits up quickly. Worked in fine yarn with a little lace detail, it also has high style. To get a close and flattering fit (and one that doesn't gape when you move), choose a size that is slightly smaller than your actual bust circumference. Wear this top alone in the summer or under a jacket when the weather turns cool.

Finished Size 27½ (30½, 35, 39½)" (70 [77.5, 89, 100.5] cm) bust circumference. *Note:* Halter is designed to measure a few inches smaller than the actual bust measurement. Halter shown measures 30½" (77.5 cm) and will fit a 34" (86.5 cm) bust.

Yarn Sportweight (#2 Fine). *Shown here:* Rowan Cashcotton 4-Ply (35% cotton, 25% polyamide, 18% angora, 13% viscose, 9% cashmere; 197 yd [180] m/50 g): #906 chintz; 3 (4, 4, 5) balls.

Needles U.S. size 3 (3.25 mm): 24" (60 cm) circular (cir). One needle smaller than size 3 for picking up sts. Adjust needle size if necessary to obtain the correct gauge.

Notions Waste yarn for provisional CO; marker (m); removable markers or safety pins; tapestry needle.

Gauge 26 stitches and 34 rows = 4" (10 cm) in stockinette stitch, worked in rounds.

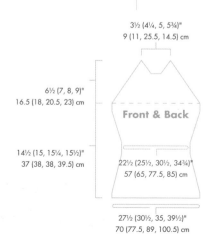

3½ (4¼, 5, 5¾)"
9 (11, 25.5, 14.5) cm

6½ (7, 8, 9)"
16.5 (18, 20.5, 23) cm

Front & Back

14½ (15, 15¼, 15½)"
37 (38, 38, 39.5) cm

22½ (25½, 30½, 34¾)"
57 (65, 77.5, 85) cm

27½ (30½, 35, 39½)"
70 (77.5, 89, 100.5) cm

Body

Using the provisional method (see Glossary), CO 178 (198, 230, 258) sts. Place marker (pm) and join for working in the rnd, being careful not to twist sts. Knit 4 rnds. **Picot rnd:** *Yo, k2tog; rep from *. Knit 4 rnds. **Next rnd:** Remove waste yarn and place exposed sts from provisional CO on smaller cir needle. Fold along picot rnd and hold needles parallel to each other with WS of knitting facing tog. With the larger right-hand needle, knit sts from the two needles tog to join hem—still 178 (198, 230, 258) sts. Cont even until piece measures 1½ (2, 2¼, 2½)" (3.8 [5, 5.5, 6.5] cm) from picot rnd. **Next rnd:** K44 (49, 57, 64), mark next st, k88 (98, 114, 128), mark next st, knit to end of rnd. **Dec rnd:** Knit to 2 sts before first marked st, ssk, k1 (marked st), k2tog, knit to 2 sts before next marked st, ssk, k1 (marked st), k2tog, knit to end—4 sts dec'd. Work 4 rnds even. Rep the last 5 rnds 7 more times—146 (166, 198, 226) sts rem. **Inc rnd:** Knit to first marked st, M1R (see Glossary), k1, M1L (see Glossary), knit to next marked st, M1R, k1, M1L, knit to end—4 sts inc'd. Work 4 rnds even. Rep the last 5 rnds 7 more times—178 (198, 230, 258) sts. Cont even until piece measures 14½ (15, 15¼, 15½)" (37 [38, 38.5, 39.5] cm) from picot edge.

DIVIDE FOR FRONT AND BACK | BO 89 (99, 115, 129) sts for back, knit to end of rnd—89 (99, 115, 129) sts rem for front. Working back and forth in rows, purl 1 (WS) row. **Dec row:** (RS) K1, ssk, knit to last 3 sts, k2tog, k1—2 sts dec'd. Dec 1 st each end of needle in this manner every RS row 7 (6, 8, 9) more times—73 (85, 97, 109) sts rem. Work triple chevron lace patt as foll:

Row 1: (RS) K1, ssk, k3, *k1, yo, ssk, k7, k2tog, yo; rep from * to last 7 sts, k4, k2tog, k1—2 sts dec'd.

Row 2 and all WS rows: Purl.

Row 3: K1, ssk, k2, *k2, yo, ssk, k5, k2tog, yo, k1; rep from * to last 6 sts, k3, k2tog, k1—2 sts dec'd.

Row 5: K1, ssk, k1, *k1, [yo, ssk] 2 times, k3, [k2tog, yo] 2 times; rep from * to last 5 sts, k2, k2tog, k1—2 sts dec'd.

Row 7: K1, ssk, *k2, [yo, ssk] 2 times, k1, [k2tog, yo] 2 times, k1; rep from * to last 4 sts, k1, k2tog, k1—2 sts dec'd.

Row 9: K1, ssk, [yo, ssk] 2 times, yo, sl 2, k1, p2sso, yo, [k2tog, yo] 2 times, *k1, [yo, ssk] 2 times, yo, sl 2, k1, p2sso, yo, [k2tog, yo] 2 times, rep from * to last 3 sts, k2tog, k1.

Row 11: K1, ssk, [yo, ssk] 2 times, k1, [k2tog, yo] 2 times, k1, *k2, [yo, ssk] 2 times, k1, [k2tog, yo] 2 times, k1; rep from * to last 14 sts, k2, [yo, ssk] 2 times, k1, [k2tog, yo] 2 times, k2tog, k1—2 sts dec'd.

Row 13: K1, [ssk, yo] 2 times, sl 2, k1, p2sso, yo, k2tog, yo, k2, *k3, yo, ssk, yo, sl 2, k1, p2sso, yo, k2tog, yo, k2; rep from * to last 13 sts, k3, yo, ssk, yo, sl 2, k1, p2sso, yo, k2tog, yo, k2tog, k1—2 sts dec'd.

Row 15: K1, ssk, yo, ssk, k1, k2tog, yo, k3, *k4, yo, ssk, k1, k2tog, yo, k3; rep from * to last 12 sts, k4, yo, ssk, k1, k2tog, yo, k2tog, k1—2 sts dec'd.

Row 17: K1, ssk, yo, sl 2, k1, p2sso, yo, k4, *k5, yo, sl 2, k1, p2sso, yo, k4; rep from * to last 11 sts, k5, yo, sl 2, k1, p2sso, yo, k2tog, k1—2 sts dec'd.

Row 18: Purl.

Dec row: (RS) K1, ssk, knit to last 3 sts, k2tog, k1—2 sts dec'd. Dec 1 st each end of needle in this manner every RS row 1 (2, 3, 5) more times—51 (61, 71, 79) sts rem.

SHAPE FRONT NECK | (WS) P19 (23, 27, 29), join a second ball of yarn and BO center 13 (15, 17, 21) sts, purl to end—19 (23, 27, 29) sts rem each side. Working each side separately, dec 1 st each end of needle every RS row 7 (9, 11, 12) times—5 sts rem each side. Work 1 WS row even. **Next row:** (RS) K1, sl 1, k2tog, psso, k1—3 sts rem each side. Work 1 WS row even. **Next row:** (RS) Sl 1, k2tog, psso—1 st rem each side. Do not cut yarn; pull ball through rem st to secure.

Finishing

FRONT NECK EDGING | With smaller cir needle, WS facing, and beg at right side of neck edge, pick up and purl (see Glossary) about 43 (57, 67, 75) sts evenly spaced along front neck edge (about 1 st in each st along sloped edges and 1 st in each BO st). Turn work so RS is facing. With size 3 (3.25 mm) needle, use a provisional method to CO 3 sts. With the yarn used for picking up sts, bring yarn behind needle and k3 CO sts. Do not turn, pull yarn tightly behind work to create I-cord. Work I-cord BO as foll: K2 from larger needle, ssk, working the last st of this needle tog with the first st of the smaller needle. Cont working I-cord BO in this manner until all picked up sts have been bound off—3 I-cord sts rem. Place these sts on holder.
Do not cut yarn.

BACK AND ARMHOLE EDGING | With smaller cir needle, WS facing, and beg at tip of point at left side of upper edge, pick up and purl about 203 (217, 253, 281) sts evenly spaced across back neck and armhole edge (about 1 st in each st along sloped edges and 1 st in each BO st). Turn work so RS is facing. With larger needle, CO 3 sts and work I-cord BO as for front, ending with 3 I-cord sts. Place sts on a holder. Do not cut yarn.

STRAPS | Remove waste yarn from provisional CO at one front point and place these sts on a needle. Place the 3 held sts on the same needle—6 sts total; yarn from I-cord BO will be in the center of these sts. Work 6-st I-cord until strap measures about 19" (48.5 cm) or desired length, tugging gently on the cord to close the gaps between sts. **Next row:** Ssk, k2, k2tog—4 sts rem. **Next row:** Ssk, k2tog—2 sts rem. **Next row:** K2tog—1 st rem. Cut yarn and pull tail through rem st to secure. Rep for other strap.

Weave in loose ends. Block to measurements.

Mohair T-Neck

LISA R. MYERS

For those of you who like a little something to wear under a suit jacket, here's a turtleneck that provides warmth without bulk. The yarn, a lightweight blend of kid mohair and silk, is used double to make an opaque body (not to mention that it knits up faster when double!) and single on large needles for a sheer trim on the lower body, cap sleeves, and neck. The result is a demure top that also looks great by itself.

Finished Size 32 (36, 40, 44, 48)" (81.5 [91.5, 101.5, 112, 122] cm) bust circumference. Sweater shown measures 36" (91.5 cm).

Yarn Fingering weight (#1 Super Fine).
Shown here: Rowan Kid Silk Haze (70% super kid mohair, 30% silk; 229 yd [210 m]/25 g): #633 violetta, 5 (5, 6, 6, 7) balls.

Needles Body—U.S. size 6 (4 mm): 24" (60 cm) circular (cir). Sleeves and edging—U.S. size 9 (5.5 mm): 24" and 16" (60 and 40 cm) cir. Adjust needle size if necessary to obtain the correct gauge.

Notions Markers (m); tapestry needle; 10 yards of a smooth sportweight yarn in a matching color for sewing seams.

Gauge 12½ stitches and 20 rows = 4" (10 cm) with single strand of yarn in stockinette stitch on larger needle, worked in the rnd; 16 stitches and 30 rows = 4" (10 cm) with double strand of yarn in stockinette stitch on smaller needle, worked in the rnd.

Notes

◎ Sweater is worked in the round in one piece to the underarms; then the front and back are worked separately to the shoulders.

◎ A smaller needle is used for the cast-on to help prevent the edge from rolling.

◎ When working with a single strand of yarn and larger needle, work the decreases and bind off loosely to prevent the fabric from puckering.

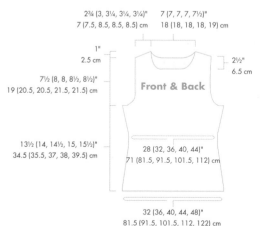

2¾ (3, 3¼, 3¼, 3¼)"
7 (7.5, 8.5, 8.5, 8.5) cm

7 (7, 7, 7, 7½)"
18 (18, 18, 18, 19) cm

1"
2.5 cm

2½"
6.5 cm

7½ (8, 8, 8½, 8½)"
19 (20.5, 20.5, 21.5, 21.5) cm

Front & Back

13½ (14, 14½, 15, 15½)"
34.5 (35.5, 37, 38, 39.5) cm

28 (32, 36, 40, 44)"
71 (81.5, 91.5, 101.5, 112) cm

32 (36, 40, 44, 48)"
81.5 (91.5, 101.5, 112, 122) cm

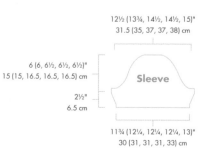

12½ (13¾, 14½, 14½, 15)"
31.5 (35, 37, 37, 38) cm

6 (6, 6½, 6½, 6½)"
15 (15, 16.5, 16.5, 16.5) cm

Sleeve

2½"
6.5 cm

11¾ (12¼, 12¼, 12¼, 13)"
30 (31, 31, 31, 33) cm

DIVIDE FOR FRONT AND BACK | BO 4 sts, knit to side-seam marker, turn work, leaving rem 64 (72, 80, 88, 96) sts unworked.

Front

Working back and forth in rows, work front as foll (rem sts will be worked later for back): BO 4 sts at beg of next 1 (1, 1, 3, 3) row(s), then dec 1 st each end of needle every RS row 3 (6, 9, 9, 12) times—50 (52, 54, 54, 56) sts rem. Work even until armholes measure 5 (5½, 5½, 6, 6)" (12.5 [14, 14, 15, 15] cm), ending with a WS row.

SHAPE NECK | K16 (17, 18, 18, 18), join second ball of yarn and BO center 18 (18, 18, 18, 20) sts, knit to end—16 (17, 18, 18, 18) sts rem each side. Working each side separately, dec 1 st at each neck edge every RS row 5 times—11 (12, 13, 13, 13) sts rem each side. Work even until armholes measure 7½ (8, 8, 8½, 8½)" (19 [20.5, 20.5, 21.5, 21.5] cm).

Shape Shoulders At each armhole edge, BO 4 (4, 5, 5, 5) sts 2 (3, 1, 1, 1) time(s), then BO 3 (0, 4, 4, 4) sts 1 (0, 2, 2, 2) time(s).

Back

With RS facing, rejoin yarn to 64 (72, 80, 88, 96) held back sts at left underarm. BO 4 sts at beg of next 2 (2, 2, 4, 4) rows, then dec 1 st each end of needle every RS row 3 (6, 9, 9, 12) times—50 (52, 54, 54, 56) sts rem. Work even until piece measures same as front to shoulder, ending with a WS row.

Body

With smaller cir needle and single strand of yarn, CO 96 (108, 120, 132, 144) sts. Change to larger cir needle and knit 1 row. Place marker (pm) and join for working in rnds, being careful not to twist sts. Work even in St st until piece measures 2½" (6.5 cm) from CO. **Inc rnd:** With smaller needle, *k3, M1 (see Glossary); rep from * to end of rnd—128 (144, 160, 176, 192) sts. Join second strand of yarn and knit 3 rnds, placing additional marker after 64th (72nd, 80th, 88th, 96th) st to denote side "seam." **Dec rnd:** [K1, k2tog, knit to 3 sts before m, ssk, k1, slip marker (sl m)] 2 times—4 sts dec'd. Knit 5 rnds, then rep dec rnd. Rep the last 6 rnds 2 more times —112 (128, 144, 160, 176) sts rem. Work even until piece measures 8 (8½, 8½, 8½, 9)" (20.5 [21.5, 21.5, 21.5, 23] cm) from CO. **Inc rnd:** *K1, M1, knit to 1 st before m, M1, k1, sl m] 2 times—4 sts inc'd. Knit 5 rnds, the rep inc rnd. Repeat the last 6 rnds 2 more times—128 (144, 160, 176, 192) sts. Work even until piece measures 13½ (14, 14½, 15, 15½)" (34.5 [35.5, 37, 38, 39.5] cm) from CO, or desired length to armhole.

SHAPE SHOULDERS AND NECK | *Note:* The shoulders and neck are shaped at the same time; read all the way through the foll instructions before proceeding. BO 4 (4, 5, 5, 5) sts at beg of next 2 rows—42 (44, 44, 44, 44, 46) sts rem. Mark center 24 (24, 24, 24, 26) sts for neck—9 (10, 10, 10, 10) sts rem for each shoulder. At each armhole edge, BO 4 (4, 0, 0, 0) sts 1 (2, 0, 0, 0) time(s), then BO 3 (0, 4, 4, 4) sts 1 (0, 2, 2, 2) time(s), and *at the same time* join a second ball of yarn and BO center 24 (24, 24, 24, 26) sts. Working each side separately (cont working shoulder shaping as established), at each neck edge dec 1 st every row (k2tog on RS row; p2tog on WS row) 2 times—no sts rem.

Sleeves (make 2)

With a single strand of yarn and smaller cir needle, CO 37 (39, 39, 39, 41) sts. Change to larger needle and work 4 rows in St st. **Inc row:** (RS) Inc 1 st each end of needle—2 sts inc'd. Work 5 rows even. Rep the last 6 rows 0 (1, 2, 2, 2) more time(s)—39 (43, 45, 45, 47) sts. Work even until piece measures 2½" (6.5 cm) from CO, ending with a WS row.

SHAPE CAP | BO 3 sts at beg of next 2 rows—33 (37, 39, 39, 41) sts rem. Dec 1 st each end of needle every RS row 13 (13, 14, 14, 14) times—7 (11, 11, 11, 13) sts rem. BO 2 (3, 3, 3, 3) sts at beg of next 2 rows—3 (5, 5, 5, 7) sts rem. BO all sts.

Finishing

With a single strand of smooth matching-color yarn threaded on a tapestry needle, sew front to back at shoulders. Sew sleeve caps into armholes. Sew sleeve and side seams. Weave in loose ends. Block lightly.

NECKBAND | With single strand of yarn, larger 16" (40 cm) cir needle, RS facing, and beg at right shoulder seam, pick up and knit 28 (28, 28, 28, 30) sts across back neck, 12 sts along left front neck edge, 18 (18, 18, 18, 20) sts across front neck, 12 sts along right front neck edge—70 (70, 70, 70, 74) sts total. Pm and join for working in rnds. Knit 1 rnd, dec 16 sts evenly spaced—54 (54, 54, 54, 58) sts rem. Work even in St st until band measures 2½" (6.5 cm) from pick-up rnd or desired total length. Loosely BO all sts. Block again if desired.

Dolman Top

LAURA GRUTZECK

The lower half of this flattering top is knitted in the usual way from the hem to the waist. The upper half is knitted side to side, beginning at one cuff and ending at the other, with short-rows worked along the way to shape the deep V-neck. The two halves meet at the waist with a bit of ribbing that extends around the neckline. Leave the neckline in a plunging V or stitch it together to the desired depth for more coverage.

Finished Size 28 (30, 34, 38)" (71 [76, 86.5, 96.5] cm) finished waist circumference and 36½ (40, 44½, 49)" (92.5 [101.5, 113, 124.5] cm) finished hip circumference. To fit 32 (34, 38, 42)" (81.5 [86.5, 96.5, 106.5] cm) bust circumference. Sweater shown measures 40" (101.5 cm) at hip.

Yarn Sportweight (#2 Fine).
Shown here: Rowan Cashsoft 4-Ply (57% merino wool, 33% microfiber, 10% cashmere; 197 yd [180 m]/50 g): #425 weather (light gray), 7 (8, 10, 12) balls.

Needles Body and sleeves—U.S. size 3 (3.25 mm). Edging—U.S. size 2 (2.75 mm): 32" (80 cm) circular (cir). Adjust needle size if necessary to obtain the correct gauge.

Notions Waste yarn for provisional CO, marker (m); removable marker or safety pin; tapestry needle.

Gauge 24 stitches and 37 rows = 4" (10 cm) in stockinette stitch worked on larger needles.

Notes
- ◎ The front and back are worked from the bottom up for the lower body; the upper body is worked sideways from cuff to cuff.
- ◎ The neck edges can be left open for a very low neckline or sewn together partway for more coverage.

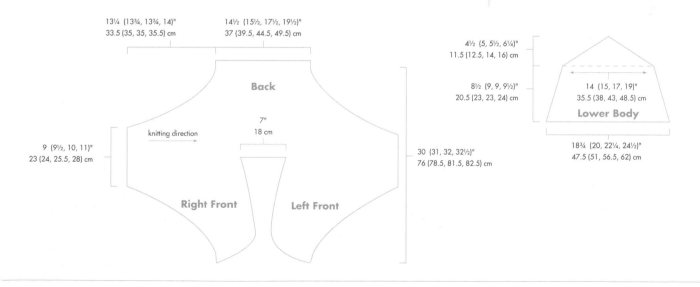

Lower Back

With larger needles and using the provisional method (see Glossary), CO 110 (120, 134, 148) sts. Work 10 rows in St st for hem facing. Knit 1 (WS) row to create turning ridge. Work 9 more rows in St st. Carefully remove waste yarn from provisional CO and place exposed sts on a smaller needle, fold facing to WS along turning ridge, and holding the needles parallel, work k2tog (1 st from each needle) across row—still 110 (120, 134, 148) sts. Work 2 rows even. **Dec row:** (RS) K1, ssk, knit to last 3 sts, k2tog, k1—2 sts dec'd. Rep dec row every 6th row 3 more times, then every 4th row 8 (10, 11, 12) times—86 (92, 104, 116) sts rem. Work even until piece measures 8½ (9, 9, 9½)" (21.5 [23, 23, 24] cm) from CO, ending with a WS row. BO all sts.

Lower Front

CO and work as for lower back until piece measures 8 (8½, 8½, 9)" (20.5 [21.5, 21.5, 23] cm) from CO, ending with a RS row—86 (92, 104, 116) sts rem. **Next row:** (WS) k1, p2tog, purl to last 3 sts, p2tog through back loops (tbl), k1—2 sts dec'd. **Next row:** K1, ssk, knit to last 3 sts, k2tog, k1—2 sts dec'd. Cont to dec 1 st each end of needle in this manner every row 40 (43, 49, 55) more times—2 sts rem; piece measures 13 (14, 14½, 15¾)" (33 [35.5, 37, 40] cm) from CO. **Next row:** K2tog—1 st rem. Fasten off rem st.

Upper Body

With smaller needle, CO 56 (58, 62, 68) sts.

RIGHT SLEEVE | Work in k1, p1 rib until piece measures 1" (2.5 cm) from CO, ending with a WS row. Change to larger needles and St st. Work 6 rows even, then inc 1 st each end of needle every RS row 54 (56, 56, 58) times—164 (170, 174, 184) sts; piece measures about 13¼ (13¾, 13¾, 14)" (33.5 [35, 35, 35.5] cm) from CO. Work 1 more WS row.

RIGHT UPPER BODY | Use the cable method (see Glossary) to CO 9 (9, 9, 6) sts at beg of next 2 rows—182 (188, 192, 196) sts. Work 2 rows even.

RIGHT FRONT | *Note:* Short-rows are introduced as decs are worked to shape the V-neck and fronts simultaneously; read all the way through the foll section before proceeding. **Dec row:** (RS) K1, ssk, knit to end—1 st dec'd. Dec 1 st at beg of every RS row 21 (23, 31, 37) more times, then every row 8 (10, 4, 0) times—30 (34, 36, 38) sts total will be dec'd. *At the same time,* after 14 (17, 22, 26) decs have been worked and 168 (171, 170, 170) sts rem, work short-rows (see Glossary) as foll: On the next WS row, work 86 (88, 90, 92) sts for back, place marker (pm), work rem 82 (83, 80, 78) sts for right front. On the foll row, work dec, knit to 5 sts before m, wrap the next st, turn work, purl to end. On the next row, work dec as established, knit to 10 sts before m, wrap next st, turn work, purl to end. Cont in this manner, working decs at beg of row as established and working 5 fewer sts every RS row before making short-row turn 10 more times—(60 sts total worked in short-row section); 152 (154, 156, 158) sts rem when all decs and short-rows have been completed; 66 sts rem on right side of m for front. Work 6 rows even, working the wraps tog with the wrapped sts.

CENTER BACK | (RS) BO 66 sts, remove m, knit to end—86 (88, 90, 92) sts rem. Work even until piece measures 7" (18 cm) from last BO row, ending with a RS row.

LEFT FRONT | (WS) Work to end of row, pm, use the cable method to CO 66 sts—152 (154, 156, 158) sts. Work 6 rows even. *Note:* Incs and short-rows are worked at the same time;

read all the way through the foll section before proceeding.
Inc row (RS): K1, M1, knit to end—1 st inc'd. Inc 1 st at front
edge every row 7 (9, 3, 0) more times, then at beg of every
RS row 22 (24, 32, 37) times—182 (188, 192, 196) sts. *At the
same time* on the first RS row, work short-rows as foll: K1,
M1, knit to 60 sts from m, wrap next st, turn, work to last st,
M1 (omit this inc for size 49" only), k1. **Next row:** Knit to
55 sts from m, wrap next st, turn, work to end. Cont in this
manner, working incs as established and working 5 more
sts every RS row before making short-row turn 10 more
times—60 sts total worked in short-row section; still 182
(188, 192, 196) sts. Work across all sts, working wraps with
wrapped sts.

LEFT UPPER BODY | Work 2 rows even—piece measures
14½ (15½, 17½, 19½)" (37 [39.5, 44.5, 49.5] cm) from CO at
cuff of right sleeve.

LEFT SLEEVE | BO 9 (9, 9, 6) sts at beg of next 2 rows—164
(170, 174, 184) sts rem. Dec 1 st each end of needle every
RS row 54 (56, 56, 58) times—56 (58, 62, 68) sts rem. Knit
6 rows even—piece measures 12¼ (12¾, 12¾, 13)" (31 [32.5,
32.5, 33] cm) from last BO. Change to smaller needle and
work k1, p1 rib for 1" (2.5 cm). Loosely BO all sts.

Finishing

Weave in loose ends. Block pieces to measurements. Fold
upper body along shoulder line and with yarn threaded on a
tapestry needle, sew sleeve seams. Sew lower front to lower
back at side seams.

UPPER BODY EDGING | With smaller cir needle, RS
facing, and beg at left side seam of upper body, pick up and
knit 88 (94, 106, 120) sts along lower edge of back, 96 (100, 102,
104) sts across front edge (pick up 1 st for each BO st), 66 sts
across back neck edge, and 96 (100, 102, 104) sts along other
front edge—346 (360, 376, 394) sts total. Place marker (pm),
and join for working in rnds. Work 1 rnd in k1, p1 rib. **Next
rnd:** Work 131 (141, 155, 171) sts, mark next st with removable

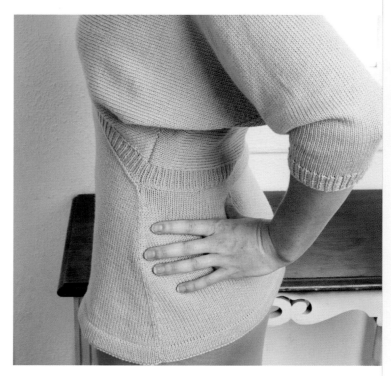

stitch marker or safety pin, work 170 sts past marked st, mark
next st, work to end of rnd—2 sts marked to indicate where
fronts will meet at center. **Next rnd:** Work to first marked st,
M1 (see Glossary), work marked st, M1, work to next marked st,
M1, work marked st, M1, work to end—4 sts inc'd. Inc in this
manner every other rnd 4 more times, working inc'd sts into rib
patt—366 (380, 396, 414) sts. BO all sts.

JOIN UPPER AND LOWER BODY | Pin marked sts
together at front and pin lower body to upper body, with
point of lower front just below marked sts at front. With
yarn threaded on a tapestry needle, sew ribbing of upper
body to lower body.

Try sweater on and check neck depth. For a higher neckline,
pin edges of neck ribbing together, starting at point of lower
front, and working up to desired height. Remove sweater,
and sew edges of neckline ribbing together as pinned.

Block again if desired.

Style

One of our goals in this book is to entice you with the versatility and fashionability of skinny yarns. Fine yarns can give you a body-hugging fit that enhances your natural curves. Fine yarns are ideal for layering, a look that's popular in contemporary fashion. Most vintage fashions and folk traditions depend on fine yarns. And just think of all the wonderful effects you can achieve with skinny yarns—sheer panels, ruffles, elegant drape—that simply are not possible with heavier yarns.

This chapter will open your eyes to the contemporary fashion, fit, and style that go hand in hand with fine yarns.

Projects

Skater Sweater

Lace-Trimmed Raglan

Wrap Dress

Bamboo Skirt

Asymmetric Cardigan

Skater Sweater

CAROL SULCOSKI

For this layered-look sweater, sportweight yarn is used to knit a short-sleeved sweater with a scoop neck. Then a contrasting fingering-weight yarn is used to knit the undersleeves (in the round to reduce the amount of finishing) that are attached to the sleeves by means of a three-needle bind-off. An optional dickey exaggerates the layered look and offers additional coverage. A decorative picot edging on the undersleeves and dickey provides a feminine touch.

Finished Size 34 (38, 42, 46)" (86.5 [96.5, 106.5, 117] cm) bust circumference. Sweater shown measures 34".

Yarn Sportweight (#2 Fine) for MC; fingering weight (#1 Super Fine) for CC. *Shown here:* Dale of Norway Svale (50% cotton, 40% viscose, 10% silk; 114 yd [104 m]/50 g): #5403 lavender (MC), 8 (8, 9, 10) balls. Dale of Norway Stork (100% cotton; 195 yd [178 m]/50 g): #0002 cream (CC), 3 (3, 4, 4) balls.

Needles Body and sleeves—U.S. size 5 (3.75 mm). Edging—U.S. size 4 (3.5 mm): straight and 16" (40 cm) circular (cir). Undersleeves and dickey—U.S. size 1 (2.25 mm): set of 4 double-pointed (dpn), 16" (40) cir, plus an extra cir needle for three-needle BO. Adjust needle size if necessary to obtain the correct gauge.

Notions Markers (m); stitch holders or waste cotton yarn; tapestry needle.

Gauge 24 stitches and 32 rows = 4" (10 cm) in reverse rice stitch pattern with MC on largest needles (for sweater body); 32 stitches and 46 rows = 4" (10 cm) in stockinette stitch with CC on smallest needles (for undersleeves and dickey).

Stitch Guide

Reverse Rice Stitch Pattern (multiple of 2 sts)
Row 1: (RS) Knit.
Row 2: *K1 through back loop (tbl), p1; rep from * to end of row.
Repeat Rows 1 and 2 for pattern.

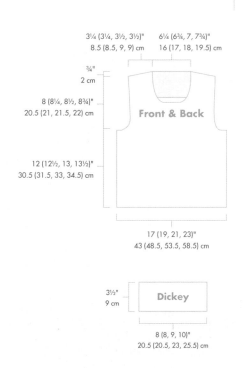

3¼ (3¼, 3½, 3½)"
8.5 (8.5, 9, 9) cm

6¼ (6¾, 7, 7¾)"
16 (17, 18, 19.5) cm

¾"
2 cm

8 (8¼, 8½, 8¾)"
20.5 (21, 21.5, 22) cm

Front & Back

12 (12½, 13, 13½)"
30.5 (31.5, 33, 34.5) cm

17 (19, 21, 23)"
43 (48.5, 53.5, 58.5) cm

3½"
9 cm

Dickey

8 (8, 9, 10)"
20.5 (20.5, 23, 25.5) cm

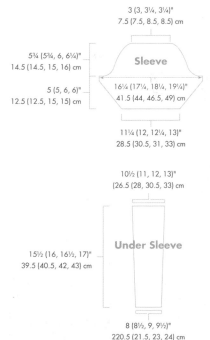

3 (3, 3¼, 3¼)"
7.5 (7.5, 8.5, 8.5) cm

5¾ (5¾, 6, 6¼)"
14.5 (14.5, 15, 16) cm

Sleeve

5 (5, 6, 6)"
12.5 (12.5, 15, 15) cm

16¼ (17¼, 18¼, 19¼)"
41.5 (44, 46.5, 49) cm

11¼ (12, 12¼, 13)"
28.5 (30.5, 31, 33) cm

10½ (11, 12, 13)"
(26.5 (28, 30.5, 33) cm

Under Sleeve

15½ (16, 16½, 17)"
39.5 (40.5, 42, 43) cm

8 (8½, 9, 9½)"
220.5 (21.5, 23, 24) cm

Note

◎ Knit the first and last stitch of every row to make sewing seams easier.

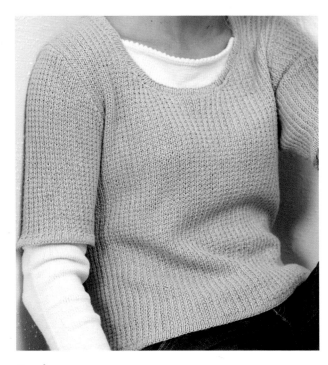

Back

With MC and middle-size straight needles, CO 104 (116, 128, 140) sts. Beg with a knit row, work 4 rows in St st. Purl 1 (RS) row for turning ridge. Beg with a purl row, work 3 rows in St st. Change to largest needles and set up patt as foll: (RS) K1 (selvedge st; knit every row), work Row 1 of reverse rice st patt (see Stitch Guide) to last st, k1 (selvedge st; knit every row). Knitting the first and last st of every row, cont in patt as established until piece measures 12 (12½, 13, 13½)" (30.5 [31.5, 33, 34.5] cm) from turning ridge, ending with a WS row.

SHAPE ARMHOLES | Keeping in patt, BO 6 (8, 9, 11) sts at beg of next 2 rows—92 (100, 110, 118) sts rem. Dec 1 st each end of needle every RS row 5 (7, 9, 10) times—82 (86, 92, 98) sts rem. Cont even until armholes measure 8 (8¼, 8½, 8¾)" (20.5 [21, 21.5, 22] cm), ending with a WS row.

SHAPE SHOULDERS | Keeping in patt, BO 7 (7, 8, 8) sts at beg of next 4 rows—54 (58, 60, 66) sts rem. **Next row:** BO 8 (9, 9, 10) sts, work next 38 (40, 42, 46) sts and place these sts on holder for back neck, BO rem 8 (9, 9, 10) sts.

Front

CO and work as for back until piece measures same length as back to armhole, ending with a WS row—104 (116, 128, 140) sts.

SHAPE ARMHOLES AND NECK | *Note:* The armholes and neck are shaped at the same time; read all the way through the next section before proceeding. Keeping in patt, BO 6 (8, 9, 11) sts at beg of next 2 rows—92 (100, 110, 118) sts rem. Dec 1 st each end of needle every RS row 5 (7, 9, 10) times and *at the same time,* when armholes measure 2 (2¼, 2½, 2¾)" (5 [5.5, 6.5, 7] cm), work to center 20 (20, 24, 28) sts, join a second ball of yarn and BO center 20 (20, 24, 28) sts, work to end. Working each side separately, dec 1 st at each neck edge every row 11 (14, 12, 13) times—20 (19, 22, 22) sts rem for each shoulder when all decs have been completed. Cont even until armholes measure 8 (8¼, 8½, 8¾)" (20.5 [21, 21.5, 22] cm), ending with a WS row.

SHAPE SHOULDERS | Keeping in patt, at each armhole edge BO 7 (7, 8, 8) sts every other row 2 times—6 (5, 6, 6) sts rem. BO all sts.

Sleeves (make 2)

With MC and middle-size straight needles, CO 68 (72, 74, 78) sts. Beg with knit row, work 4 rows in St st. Purl 1 (RS) row for turning ridge. Beg with a purl row, work 3 rows in St st. Change to largest needles and work in reverse rice st patt, inc 1 st each end of needle every other row 11 (13, 17, 19) times, then every 4th row 4 (3, 1, 0) time(s)—98 (104, 110, 116) sts. Cont even in patt until piece measures 5 (5, 6, 6)" (12.5 [12.5, 15, 15] cm) from turning ridge, ending with a WS row.

SHAPE CAP | BO 6 (8, 9, 11) sts at beg of next 2 rows—86 (88, 92, 94) sts rem. Dec 1 st each end of needle every RS row 5 (7, 9, 10) times, then every row 12 (13, 13, 14) times, then every RS row 9 (7, 6, 5) more times—34 (34, 36, 36) sts rem. BO 4 sts at beg of next 4 rows—18 (18, 20, 20) sts rem. BO rem sts.

Undersleeves (make 2)

With CC and smallest dpn, CO 64 (68, 72, 76) sts. Arrange sts evenly on 3 dpn, place marker (pm), and join for working in rnds, being careful not to twist sts. Knit 4 rnds. **Picot rnd:** K1, *yo, k2tog; rep from * to last st, k1. Cont to knit every rnd until piece measures 2 (2, 2½, 3)" (5 [5, 6.5, 7.5] cm) from picot rnd. **Inc rnd:** K1, M1L (see Glossary), knit to last 3 sts, M1R (see Glossary), k2—2 sts inc'd. Work 11 (11, 9, 9) rnds even. Rep the last 12 (12, 10, 10) rnds 9 (9, 11, 13) more times, changing to cir needle when there are too many sts to fit on dpn—84 (88, 96, 104) sts. Cont even until piece measures 15½ (16, 16½, 17)" (39.5 [40.5, 42, 43] cm) from picot rnd. Place sts on holder or cotton waste yarn.

Dickey (optional)

With CC and smallest needles, CO 64 (64, 72, 80) sts. Work 4 rows in St st. **Picot row:** (RS) K1, *yo, k2tog; rep from * to last st, k1. Cont even in St st until piece measures 3½" (9 cm) or desired length from picot row, ending with a WS row. BO all sts.

Finishing

Weave in loose ends. Block pieces to measurements. With MC threaded on a tapestry needle, sew front to back at shoulders. Sew sleeve caps into armholes. Sew sleeve and side seams. Turn up bottom hem and sew in place.

NECKBAND | With MC, middle-size cir needle, RS facing, and beg at right shoulder seam, pick up and knit 42 (44, 48, 50) sts along right front neck to center front, 42 (44, 48, 50) sts from center front to left shoulder seam, then k38 (40, 42, 46) held back neck sts—122 (128, 138, 146) sts total. Pm and join for working in rnds. Knit 4 rnds, purl 1 rnd for turning ridge, knit 4 rnds. BO all sts. Fold neckband to WS along turning ridge and sew in place.

UNDERSLEEVES | Fold lower edge of undersleeves along picot rnd and sew facing to WS. Turn up and sew sleeve hems in the same fashion. Turn up the hem of the outer sleeve, wrong side out, to give access to the underside of the hem. With spare ball of CC, rem small cir needle, and WS of sleeve facing, pick up and knit about 84 (99, 96, 104) sts evenly spaced along CO edge of hemmed sleeve, making sure the fabric does not pucker or ruffle. If necessary, knit 1 rnd, inc or dec evenly spaced as needed to result in 84 (99, 96, 104) sts. Being careful to align undersleeve with hemmed sleeve, use the three-needle method (see Glossary) to BO live sts tog. Turn hem of outer sleeve down to cover three-needle BO.

DICKEY | Fold top edge of dickey to form picot edge and tack down to WS. With MC threaded on a tapestry needle, sew RS of dickey to WS of front neck.

Lace-Trimmed Raglan

CAROL SULCOSKI

This sweater exemplifies simple elegance, with clean raglan lines and a delicate lace edging at the hem, cuffs, and neckline. A single repeat of the same lace motif continues in a thin stripe along the sleeves from the cuffs to the shoulders where it narrows as it intersects with the raglan shaping. Knitted in a soft fine wool yarn, this lightweight sweater is comfortable right next to the skin.

Finished Size 34¼ (37¾, 42, 46¼)" (87 [96, 106.5, 117.5] cm bust circumference. Sweater shown measures 34¼" (87 cm).

Yarn Fingering weight (#1 Super Fine). *Shown here:* Rowan 4-Ply Soft (100% wool; 191 yd [175 m]/50 g): #393 linseed, 8 balls.

Needles Body and sleeves—size U.S. 3 (3.25 mm): 16" and 24" (40 and 60 cm) circular (cir) and set of 4 or 5 double-pointed (dpn). Edging—size U.S. 2 (3 mm): 24" (60 cm) cir and set of 4 or 5 dpn. Adjust needle size if necessary to obtain the correct gauge.

Notions Markers (m); stitch holders; tapestry needle.

Gauge 28 stitches and 36 rows = 4" (10 cm) in stockinette stitch worked in the round on larger needles.

Notes

◎ The body is knitted in the round to the armholes, then the sleeves (also knitted in the round) are joined, and the yoke is knitted in the round to the neck, at which point the stitches are worked back and forth in rows to shape the back neck; be sure to adapt the lace pattern for working in rows instead of rounds at this point, working Row 2 of lace pattern as p1, *k5, p1; rep from *.

◎ The sleeve increases are worked near the beginning/end of the round where they will be less noticeable. The lace motif extends along the center of the sleeve from the cuff to the shoulder, then to the neck. When working the yoke shaping, if there are too few stitches to complete a full repeat of the lace panel at the center of the sleeve, switch the first and last repeats to stockinette stitch, continuing the center lace motif.

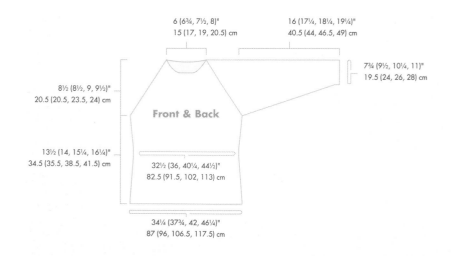

6 (6¾, 7½, 8)"
15 (17, 19, 20.5) cm

16 (17¼, 18¼, 19¼)"
40.5 (44, 46.5, 49) cm

7¾ (9½, 10¼, 11)"
19.5 (24, 26, 28) cm

8½ (8½, 9, 9½)"
20.5 (20.5, 23.5, 24) cm

Front & Back

13½ (14, 15¼, 16¼)"
34.5 (35.5, 38.5, 41.5) cm

32½ (36, 40¼, 44½)"
82.5 (91.5, 102, 113) cm

34¼ (37¾, 42, 46¼)"
87 (96, 106.5, 117.5) cm

Body

With longer smaller cir needle, CO 240 (264, 294, 324) sts. Place marker (pm) and join for working in rnds, being careful not to twist sts. Work all sts according to Lace chart until piece measures 1½ (1½, 2, 2)" (3.8 [3.8, 5, 5] cm) from CO. Change to St st and pm after 120 (132, 147, 162) sts to denote side "seam"—120 (132, 147, 162) sts each for front and back. **Dec rnd:** K2, k2tog, knit to 4 sts before m, ssk, k2, slip marker (sl m), k2, k2tog, knit to 4 sts before end of rnd m, ssk, k2—4 sts dec'd. Cont even until piece measures 6½ (6½, 7½, 8)" (16.5 [16.5, 19, 20.5] cm) from CO. Rep dec rnd. Cont even until piece measures 7½ (7½, 8½, 9)" (19 [19, 21.5, 23] cm) from CO. Rep dec rnd once more—228 (252, 282, 312) sts rem. Cont even until piece measures 8½ (8½, 9½, 10)" (21.5 [21.5, 24, 25.5] cm) from CO. **Inc rnd:** K2, M1L (see Glossary), knit to 2 sts before m, M1R (see Glossary), k2, sl m, k2, M1L, knit to 2 sts before m, M1R, k2—4 sts inc'd. Cont even until piece measures 9½ (9½, 10½, 11)" (24 [24, 26.5, 28] cm) from CO. Rep inc rnd. Cont even until piece measures 10½ (10½, 11½, 12)" (26.5 [26.5, 29, 30.5] cm) from CO. Rep inc rnd once more—240 (264, 294, 324) sts. Cont even until piece measures 13½ (14, 15¼, 16¼)" (34.5 [35.5, 38.5, 41.5] cm) from CO, ending 5 (7, 7, 10) sts before end of rnd m.

DIVIDE FOR FRONT AND BACK | BO 5 (7, 7, 10) sts, remove m, BO 5 (7, 7, 10) more sts, knit to 5 (7, 7, 10) sts before next m, BO 10 (14, 14, 20) sts (removing m when you come to it), knit to end—220 (236, 266, 284) sts rem; 110 (118, 133, 142) sts each for front and back. Set aside.

SLEEVES (MAKE 2) | With smaller dpn, CO 54 (66, 72, 78) sts. Pm and join for working in rnds, being careful not to twist sts. Work all sts according to Lace chart until piece measures 1½ (1½, 2, 2)" (3.8 [3.8, 5, 5] cm) from CO. Change to larger dpn. **Next row:** K18 (24, 27, 30), pm, work next 18 sts in lace patt as established, pm, k18 (24, 27, 30). Cont working the center 18 sts in lace patt as established and other sts in St st, work even for 3 rnds. **Inc rnd:** K2, M1L, work as established to last 2 sts, M1R, k2—2 sts inc'd. Work 5 rnds even. Rep the shaping of the last 6 rnds 16 (4, 6, 13) more times, changing to shorter cir needle when there are too many sts to fit on dpn. Then work inc rnd every 8th rnd 0 (10, 11, 6) times—88 (96, 108, 118) sts. Cont even until piece measures 16 (17¼, 18¼, 19¼)" (40.5 [44, 46.5, 49] cm) from CO, ending 5 (7, 7, 10) sts from end of rnd on last rnd. **Next rnd:** Removing markers when you come to them, BO 10 (14, 14, 20) sts, work to end—78 (82, 94, 98) sts rem. Place sts on holder.

Yoke

With larger cir needle, RS facing, and maintaining patt as established, work 78 (82, 94, 98) sts for one sleeve, pm, k110 (118, 133, 142) front sts, pm, work 78 (82, 94, 98) sts for other sleeve, pm, k110 (118, 133, 142) back sts, pm, and join for working in rnds—376 (400, 454, 480) sts total. Work 4 rnds even. **Dec rnd:** *K2, k2tog, knit to 4 sts before next m, ssk, k2, sl m; rep from * 3 more times—8 sts dec'd; 368 (392, 446, 472) sts rem. Work 1 rnd even. Rep the shaping of the last 2 rnds 33 (33, 38, 40) more times and *at the same time,* when piece measures 4½ (4½, 5, 5)" (11.5 [11.5, 12.5, 12.5] cm) from joining rnd, shape neck as foll.

SHAPE NECK | Cont working decs as established, work to center 20 (20, 20, 24) sts of front, knit these sts, then place them on a holder, work to end of rnd. Cut off yarn. From here on, work back and forth in rows (see Notes). Rejoin yarn at left front neck edge and work 1 WS row even. BO 2 (3, 3, 3) sts at beg of next 4 (2, 4, 4) rows, then BO 0 (2, 2, 2) sts at beg of next 0 (4, 4, 4) rows. **Next row:** (RS) Dec 1 st at neck edge, work to sleeve m, sl m, work in St st to center 6 sts, work 6 sts in lace patt as established, work in St st to next marker,

sl m, knit to next sleeve m, k6, work 6 sts in lace patt as established, k6, sl m, knit to end—1 st dec'd. **Next row:** (WS) Dec 1 st at neck edge, work in patt as established to end—1 st dec'd. Dec 1 st at beg of the next 8 (6, 4, 6) rows—66 (86, 96, 100) sts rem when all armhole and neck decs have been worked. Cont even if necessary until armholes measures 8½ (8½, 9, 9½)" (21.5 [21.5, 23, 24] cm), ending with a WS row. Cut yarn.

Finishing

NECKBAND | With smaller cir needle and RS facing, rejoin yarn at the first st after the 6-st lace patt on the right shoulder. Cont in lace stripe patt as established, work across rem 4 (5, 4, 5) right sleeve sts, 42 (48, 53, 56) back sts, 14 (16, 14, 16) left sleeve sts, pick up and knit 30 (32, 31, 32) sts along left front neck edge, k20 (20, 20, 24) held front neck sts, pick up and knit 30 (31, 30, 31) sts along right front neck edge, work 4 sleeve sts, and 6 sts from center of right sleeve—150 (162, 162, 174) sts total. Pm and join for working in rnds. Work in lace patt until neckband measures 1" (2.5 cm) from pick-up rnd. BO all sts in patt.

Weave in loose ends. Block to measurements. With yarn threaded on a tapestry needle, sew underarm seams.

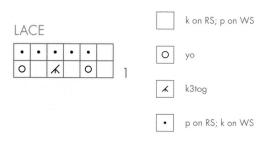

LACE

	k on RS; p on WS
	yo
	k3tog
	p on RS; k on WS

Wrap Dress

LAURA GRUTZECK

Worked in a fingering-weight yarn and a body-conforming silhouette, this knitted dress is as flattering as it is comfortable. The lightweight silk-wool yarn used here is marketed for hard-wearing socks, but it imparts an attractive drape and swing in the skirt and makes for easy laundering. Designed in a classic wrap style, this dress is flattering on a variety of body types.

Finished Size 30½ (33½, 35½, 37½, 41½)" (77.5 [85, 90, 95, 105.5] cm) bust circumference. Dress shown measures 33½" (85 cm). *Note:* The sizing is flexible due to the wrap style; choose a size the same as or smaller than your actual bust measurement.

Yarn Fingering weight (#1 Super Fine). *Shown here:* Regia Silk (55% wool, 20% silk, 25% nylon; 219 yd [200 m]/50 g): #71 loden (MC), 13 (15, 17, 19, 23) balls; #30 red (CC), 2 (2, 2, 3, 3) balls.

Needles Body and sleeves—U.S. size 3 (3.25 mm): 32" (80 cm) circular (cir). Trim—U.S. size 2 (2.75 mm). Adjust needle size if necessary to obtain the correct gauge.

Notions Stitch holders or waste yarn; tapestry needle.

Gauge 28 stitches and 38 rows = 4" (10 cm) in stockinette stitch on larger needle.

Notes

◎ The skirt is worked from the waist down; the bodice is worked from the waist up.

◎ Knit the first and last stitch of every row for selvedge stitches.

◎ Work all increases 1 stitch in from the selvedge edge. Work increases as M1R at beg of rows and as M1L at end of rows.

◎ Work all decreases 1 stitch in from the selvedge edge. Work decreases as ssk at the beginning of right-side rows and as k2tog at the end of right-side rows; work decreases as p2tog at the beginning of wrong-side rows and as p2tog tbl at the end of wrong-side rows.

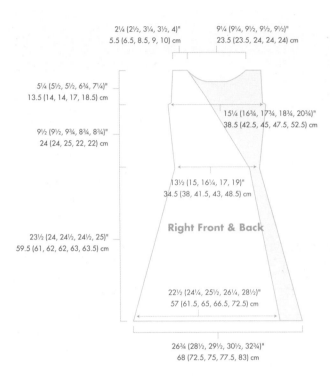

2¼ (2½, 3¼, 3½, 4)"
5.5 (6.5, 8.5, 9, 10) cm

9¼ (9¼, 9½, 9½, 9½)"
23.5 (23.5, 24, 24, 24) cm

5¼ (5½, 5½, 6¾, 7¼)"
13.5 (14, 14, 17, 18.5) cm

15¼ (16¾, 17¾, 18¾, 20¾)"
38.5 (42.5, 45, 47.5, 52.5) cm

9½ (9½, 9¾, 8¾, 8¾)"
24 (24, 25, 22, 22) cm

13½ (15, 16¼, 17, 19)"
34.5 (38, 41.5, 43, 48.5) cm

Right Front & Back

23½ (24, 24½, 24½, 25)"
59.5 (61, 62, 62, 63, 63.5) cm

22½ (24¼, 25½, 26¼, 28½)"
57 (61.5, 65, 66.5, 72.5) cm

26¾ (28½, 29½, 30½, 32¾)"
68 (72.5, 75, 77.5, 83) cm

2¼ (2¼, 2¼, 2½ 2½)"
5.5 (5.5, 5.5, 6.5, 6.5) cm

5 (5½, 5¾, 6, 6½)"
12.5 (14, 14.5, 15, 16.5) cm

Sleeve

11¾ (12¼, 13¼, 13¾, 14¼)"
30 (31,33.5, 35, 36) cm

12 (12½, 12½, 13, 13½)"
30.5 (31.5, 31.5, 33, 34.5) cm

8¾ (9¼, 9½, 10, 10½)"
22 (23.5, 24, 25.5, 26.5) cm

Skirt Back

With MC and larger needle, CO 95 (105, 113, 119, 133) sts. Knitting the first and last st of every row for selvedge sts, work center 93 (103, 111, 117, 131) sts in St st for 10 rows. Inc row: (RS) K1, M1R (see Glossary), knit to last st, M1L (see Glossary), k1—2 sts inc'd. Work 3 rows even. Rep the last 4 rows 37 more times—171 (181, 189, 195, 209) sts. Rep inc row, then work 5 rows even. Rep the last 6 rows 7 (8, 8, 8, 9) more times—187 (199, 207, 213, 229) sts. Cont even until piece measures 23½ (24, 24½, 24½, 25)" (59.5 [61, 62, 62, 63.5] cm) from CO, ending with a RS row. Knit 1 (WS) row for turning ridge. Work 8 rows even in St st for facing. Place sts on holder or waste yarn.

Skirt Left Front

With MC and larger needle, CO 83 (93, 101, 107, 121) sts. Set-up row: (RS) K5, p1, knit to end. Knit the first and last st of every row for selvedge sts and work the 6th st from the beg of RS rows in rev St st (purl on RS; knit on WS) throughout to form a turning ridge. Work 5 rows even in St st. *Note:* Incs are worked at center front at the same time as incs are introduced at side-seam edge; read all the way through the foll section before proceeding. Inc row: (RS) K5, p1, k2, M1R, knit to end—1 st inc'd. Work 5 rows even. Rep the last 6 rows 15 more times. Rep inc row, then work 7 rows even. Rep the last 8 rows 12 (13, 13, 13, 13) more times. *At the same time,* after 10 rows have been worked, inc 1 st at end of RS row (knit to last st, M1L, k1) every 4th row 38 times, then every 6th row 8 (9, 9, 9, 10) times—158 (170, 178, 184, 199) sts after all incs have been worked. Cont even until piece measures 22½ (23, 23½, 23½, 24)" (57 [58.5, 59.5, 59.5, 61] cm) from CO, ending with a RS row. Beg with the next (WS) row, work short-rows (see Glossary) as foll:

Short-Row 1: K1, p147 (159, 167, 173, 188), wrap next st, turn work, knit to end.

Short-Row 2: K1, p137 (149, 157, 163, 178) sts, wrap next st, turn, knit to end.

Cont in this manner, knitting 10 fewer sts each short-row 3 more times—108 (120, 128, 134, 149) sts worked on last short-row. **Next row:** (WS) Work across all sts, working wraps tog with wrapped sts. Work 1 RS row even. Knit 1 (WS) row for turning ridge. **Next row:** BO 6 sts, knit to end—152 (164, 172, 178, 193) sts rem. Work 7 more rows in St st. Place sts on holder or waste yarn.

Skirt Right Front

With MC and larger needle, CO 83 (93, 101, 107, 121) sts. **Set-up row:** (RS) K77 (87, 95, 101, 115), p1, k5. Knit the first and last st of every row for selvedge sts and work 6th st from the end of RS rows in rev St st throughout to form turning ridge. Work 5 rows even in St st. *Note:* Incs are worked at center front at the same time as incs are worked at side-seam edge; read all the way through the foll section before proceeding. **Inc row:** (RS) Work to last 8 sts, M1L, k2, p1, k5—1 st inc'd. Work 5 rows even. Rep the last 6 rows 15 more times. Rep inc row, then work 7 rows even. Rep the last 8 rows 12 (13, 13, 13, 13) more times. *At the same time,* after 10 rows have been worked, inc 1 st at beg of RS row (k1, M1R) every 4th row 38 times, then every 6th row 8 (9, 9, 9, 10) times—158 (170, 178, 184, 199) sts after all incs have been worked. Cont even until piece measures 22½ (23, 23½, 23½, 24)" (57 [58.5, 59.5, 59.5, 61] cm) from CO, ending with a WS row. Beg with the next (RS) row, work short-rows as foll:

Short-Row 1: K148 (160, 168, 174, 189), wrap next st, turn, purl to last st, k1.

Short-Row 2: K138 (150, 158, 164, 179), wrap next st, turn, purl to last st, k1.

Cont in this manner, knitting 10 fewer sts each short-row 3 more times—108 (120, 128, 134, 149) sts worked on last short-row. **Next row:** (RS) Work across all sts, working wraps tog with wrapped sts. Knit 1 (WS) row for turning ridge. Work 1 RS row even. **Next row:** (WS) BO 6 sts, purl to end—152 (164, 172, 178, 193) sts rem. Work 6 more rows in St st. Place sts on holder or waste yarn.

Bodice Back

With MC and larger needle, CO 95 (105, 113, 119, 133) sts. Knitting the first and last st of every row for selvedge sts, work center 93 (103, 111, 117, 131) sts in St st until piece measures 1" (2.5 cm) from CO, ending with a WS row. Inc row: (RS) K1, M1R, knit to last st, M1L, k1—2 sts inc'd. Work 11 rows even. Rep the last 12 rows 5 more times—107 (117, 125, 131, 145) sts. Cont even until piece measures 9½ (9½, 9¾, 8¾, 8¾)" (24 [24, 25, 22, 22] cm) from CO, ending with a WS row.

SHAPE ARMHOLES | BO 4 (6, 6, 6, 7) sts at beg of next 2 rows—99 (105, 113, 119, 131) sts rem. Dec 1 st each end of needle every RS row 1 (2, 1, 1, 3) time(s)—97 (101, 111, 117, 125) sts rem. Cont even until armholes measure 5¼ (5½, 5½, 6¾, 7¼)" (14 [14, 14, 17, 18.5] cm), ending with a WS row.

SHAPE NECK | With RS facing, k22 (24, 28, 31, 34), join a second ball of yarn and BO center 53 (53, 55, 55, 57) sts, knit to end—22 (24, 28, 31, 34) sts rem each side. Working each side separately, cont knitting the first and last st of every row and dec 1 st at each neck edge every RS row 6 times—16 (18, 22, 25, 28) sts rem. Place sts on holders or waste yarn.

Bodice Right Front

With MC and larger needle, CO 80 (90, 98, 104, 118) sts. Knitting the first and last st of every row, work center 78 (88, 96, 102, 116) sts in St st. *Note:* The center front, side seam, and armhole are shaped at the same time; read all the way through the foll sections before proceeding. Dec 1 st at beg of every RS row (center front) 65 (70, 73, 71, 71) times, then every row 0 (0, 2, 7, 15) times. *At the same time,* when piece measures 1" (2.5 cm) from CO, inc 1 st at end of next RS row, then every 12th row 5 more times. Cont even until piece measures 9½ (9½, 9¾, 8¾, 8¾)" (24 [24, 25, 22, 22] cm) from CO, ending with a RS row.

SHAPE ARMHOLE | (WS) BO 4 (6, 6, 6, 7) sts, work to end of row, working decs as established. Dec 1 st at armhole edge every RS row 1 (2, 1, 1, 3) time(s)—16 (18, 22, 25, 28) sts rem when all incs and decs have been completed. Cont even until piece measures same as back to shoulder. Place sts on holder or waste yarn.

Bodice Left Front

With MC and larger needle, CO 80 (90, 98, 104, 118) sts. Knitting the first and last st of every row, work center 78 (88, 96, 102, 116) sts in St st. *Note:* The center front, side seam, and armhole are shaped at the same time; read all the way through the foll sections before proceeding. Dec 1 st at end of every RS row (center front) 65 (70, 73, 71, 71) times, then every row 0 (0, 2, 7, 15) times. *At the same time*, when piece measures 1" (2.5 cm) from CO, inc 1 st at the beginning of next RS row, then every 12th row 5 more times. Cont even until piece measures 9½ (9½, 9¾, 8¾, 8¾)" (24 [24, 25, 22, 22] cm) from CO, ending with a WS row.

SHAPE ARMHOLE | (RS) BO 4 (6, 6, 6, 7) sts, work to end of row, working decs as established. Dec 1 st at armhole edge every RS row 1 (2, 1, 1, 3) time(s)—16 (18, 22, 25, 28) sts rem when all incs and decs have been completed. Cont even until piece measures same as back to shoulder. Place sts on holder or waste yarn.

Sleeves (make 2)

With MC, larger needle, and using the provisional method (see Glossary), CO 62 (64, 66, 70, 74) sts. Knit the first and last st of every row for selvedge sts; work center 60 (62, 64, 68, 72) sts in St st. Beg with a WS row, work 8 rows even. Knit 1 WS row for turning ridge. Work 8 rows even. **Next row:** Remove waste yarn from provisional CO and place exposed CO sts on a separate needle. Fold the piece along the turning ridge, hold the two needles parallel to each other, and with RS facing, knit 1 row, working the sts from the two needles tog—still 62 (64, 66, 70, 74) sts. Cont even until piece measures 2" (5 cm) from turning ridge, ending with a WS row. **Inc row:** (RS) Inc 1 st each end of needle every 6th row 0 (0, 8, 4, 3) times, then every 8th row 10 (11, 5, 9, 10) times—82 (86, 92, 96, 100) sts. Cont even until piece measures 12 (12½, 12½, 13, 13½)" (30.5 [31.5, 31.5, 33, 34.5] cm) from turning ridge, ending with a WS row.

SHAPE CAP | BO 4 (6, 6, 6, 7) sts at beg of next 2 rows—74 (74, 80, 84, 86) sts rem. Dec 1 st each end of needle every RS row 18 (21, 20, 23, 25) times, then every row 11 (8, 12, 10, 9) times—16 (16, 16, 18, 18) sts rem. BO all sts.

Belt and Neck Trim

With CC and smaller needle, CO 14 sts. Work k1, p1 rib until piece measures 43 (43, 44, 46, 50)" (109 [109, 112, 117, 127] cm) from CO. Work short-rows to shape neck trim bodice as foll:

Short-Row 1: Work 12 sts, wrap next st, turn, work to end.

Short-Row 2: Work 10 sts, wrap next st, turn, work to end.

Cont in this manner, working 2 sts fewer every short-row until 2 sts rem, turn, work to end. **Next row:** Work across all sts, working wraps tog with wrapped sts. **Next row:** Work to last st, M1, work last st—15 sts. Knit the new st every row; it is a selvedge st that will be used to attach the trim to the bodice. Cont even until piece measures 14" (35.5 cm) from the last short-row turn. Inc 1 st inside the selvedge st (i.e., work to selvedge st, M1, knit selvedge st) every other row 18 times—33 sts. Cont even until piece measures 18¼ (18½, 18¾, 19, 19½)" (46.5 [47, 47.5, 48.5, 49.5] cm) from the last short-row turn. Mark the selvedge stitch edge for shoulder placement. Beg with a row that starts with the selvedge st, work short-rows as foll:

Short-Row 1: Work 29 sts, wrap next st, turn, work to end.

Short-Row 2: Work 25 sts, wrap next st, turn, work to end.

Cont in this manner, working 4 sts fewer every short-row until 5 sts rem, turn, work to end. **Next row:** Work across all sts, working wraps tog with wrapped sts. Cont even until piece measures 7¾ (7¾, 8, 8, 8)" (19.5 [19.5, 20.5, 20.5, 20.5] cm) from shoulder marker. Beg with a row that begins with a selvedge st, work short-rows as foll:

Short-Row 1: Work 5 sts, wrap next st, turn, work to end.

Short-Row 2: Work 9 sts, wrap next st, turn, work to end.

Cont in this manner, working 4 more sts every short-row until all sts have been worked, working wraps tog with wrapped sts. Cont even until piece measures 9¾ (9¾, 10, 10, 10)" (25 [25, 25.5, 25.5, 25.5] cm) from previous shoulder marker. Mark selvedge edge for other shoulder placement. Work 10 rows even. Dec 1 st every other row 18 times as foll: Work to 2 sts before selvedge st, k2tog, k1 (selvedge st)—15 sts rem after all decs have been worked. Cont even

until piece measures 18 (18¼, 18½, 18¾, 19¼)" (45.5 [46.5, 47, 47.5, 49] cm) from last shoulder marker.

Beg with a row that begins with the selvedge st, work short-rows as foll:

Short-Row 1: Work 3 sts, wrap next st, turn, work to end.

Short-Row 2: Work 5 sts, wrap next st, turn, work to end.

Cont in this manner, working 2 more sts every short-row until all sts have been worked, working wraps tog with wrapped sts. **Next row:** Work to last 2 sts, k2tog—14 sts rem (this eliminates the selvedge st). Cont even until piece measures 43 (43, 44, 46, 50)" (109 [109, 112, 117, 127] cm) from last short-row turn. BO all sts in patt.

Finishing

Place held bodice front and back sts on needles and with RS facing tog, use the three-needle method (see Glossary) to BO shoulder sts tog. With MC threaded on a tapestry needle, sew bodice back to skirt back. Fold the front edges of the skirt to the inside along the vertical purl ridge. Steam-block in place.

Beg at side seams, sew bodice fronts to skirt fronts, leaving the last few sts of the skirt free so that the front edge of the skirt can roll to the WS. Tack front edge facing in place, if desired. With CC threaded on a tapestry needle and using a mattress st (see Glossary), sew selvedge st of trim to selvedge st of bodice fronts, matching shoulder markers to shoulder seams of bodice, and matching the points of the first and last short-row turns with the bottom edges of the bodice fronts. Sew sleeve caps into armholes. Sew sleeve and side seams, leaving 1" (2.5 cm) open above waist seam on right or left side for tie to pass through. Fold hem of skirt to WS along turning ridge and sew in place.

Weave in loose ends. Block to measurements.

Bamboo | Skirt

LISA R. MYERS

You'll find this skirt easy to knit—there's very little counting involved and the wool/bamboo-blend yarn is a treat to work with besides being the perfect combination for a skirt. The "bounce" of the wool causes the stitches to hold their shape, and the drape of the bamboo imparts a graceful silhouette that doesn't cling. If you prefer a shorter or longer skirt, simply cast on fewer or more stitches and adjust the number of stitches in the first three marked sections of the row accordingly.

Finished Size 25½ (28, 31, 33½, 36)" (65 [71, 78.5, 85, 91.5] cm) waist circumference and 32 (36, 37½, 40½, 43½)" (81.5 [91.5, 95, 103, 110.5] cm) hip circumference. Skirt shown measures 28" (71 cm) at waist. *Note:* This skirt is designed for a body-hugging fit; it will stretch when worn.

Yarn Sportweight (#2 Fine).
Shown here: Classic Elite Wool Bamboo (50% wool, 50% bamboo; 118 yds [108 m]/50 g): #1678 chestnut, 6 (6, 7, 7, 8) balls.

Needles U.S. size 6 (4 mm): 24" (60 cm) circular (cir). Adjust needle size if necessary to obtain the correct gauge.

Notions Waste yarn for provisional CO; removable stitch markers or safety pins (m); tapestry needle; 1½ yd (1.4 meter) ½" (1.3 cm) wide grosgrain or decorative ribbon.

Gauge 22 stitches and 28 rows = 4" (10 cm) in stockinette stitch.

◎ Skirt is worked side to side and shaped with short-rows. The two ends are joined with Kitchener stitch.

◎ A slip-stitch turning ridge marks the fold line for the casing at the waistband.

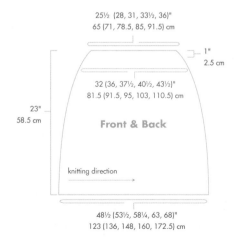

25½ (28, 31, 33½, 36)"
65 (71, 78.5, 85, 91.5) cm

1"
2.5 cm

32 (36, 37½, 40½, 43½)"
81.5 (91.5, 95, 103, 110.5) cm

23"
58.5 cm

Front & Back

knitting direction

48½ (53½, 58¼, 63, 68)"
123 (136, 148, 160, 172.5) cm

Skirt

Using the provisional method (see Glossary), CO 126 sts and *at the same time* mark the 20th, 40th, 60th, 80th, 100th, and 121st sts with removable markers (to help keep track of short-row turns). Work short-rows (see Glossary) as foll:

Row 1: K120, slip 1 purlwise with yarn in back (wyb), k5.

Row 2: Purl to last 2 sts, k2.

Row 3: K60, wrap next st, turn work.

Row 4: Knit.

Rows 5 and 6: Rep Rows 1 and 2.

Row 7: K100, wrap next st, turn.

Row 8: Knit.

Rows 9 and 10: Rep Rows 1 and 2.

Row 11: K40, wrap next st, turn.

Row 12: Knit.

Rows 13 and 14: Rep Rows 1 and 2.

Row 15: K80, wrap next st, turn.

Row 16: Knit.

Rows 17 and 18: Rep Rows 1 and 2.

Row 19: K60, wrap next st, turn.

Row 20: Knit.

Rows 21 and 22: Rep Rows 1 and 2.

Row 23: K100, wrap next st, turn.

Row 24: Knit.

Rows 25 and 26: Rep Rows 1 and 2.

Row 27: K40, wrap next st, turn.

Row 28: Knit.

Rows 29–32: Rep Rows 1 and 2 twice.

Row 33: K20, wrap next st, turn.

Row 34: Knit.

Rep these 34 rows 9 (10, 11, 12, 13) more times and *at the same time* work a buttonhole on Row 25 of final repeat as foll: k120, sl 1 pwise wyb, BO next 3 sts, k2. On the foll row, p1, use the backward loop method (see Glossary) to CO 3 sts over gap, purl to end.

Finishing

Carefully remove waste yarn from provisional CO and place live sts on a spare needle. With yarn threaded on a tapestry needle, use the Kitchener st (see Glossary) to graft the exposed CO sts to the working sts to form a tube. Fold waistband along slip-stitch turning ridge to WS and sew in place to form casing for ribbon. Beg and end at buttonhole, insert ribbon through casing. Weave in loose ends. Wet- or steam-block.

Asymmetric Cardigan

LAURA GRUTZECK

A diagonal front closure adds an interesting twist to this otherwise classic cardigan. The body and sleeves are worked from the bottom up in a lightly textured moss stitch and edged with ribbing. A few short-rows are used to raise the back neck (and give a more comfortable fit). Knitted in a wool/cotton-blend yarn, this cardigan can be worn throughout the year.

Finished Size 33½ (36, 41½, 46½)" 85 [91.5, 105.5, 118) bust circumference, buttoned. Sweater shown measures 36" (91.5 cm).

Yarn Sportweight (#2 Fine).
Shown here: Blackberry Ridge Cotton Blend (80% wool, 20% cotton; 325 yd [297 m] 4 oz): gray cloud, 4 (5, 5, 6) skeins.

Needles U.S. size 5 (3.75mm): 32" (80 cm) circular. Adjust needle size if necessary to obtain the correct gauge.

Notions Tapestry needle; eight ¾" (2 cm) buttons.

Gauge 22 stitches and 32 rows = 4" (10 cm) in moss stitch.

Stitch Guide

Moss Stitch (even number of sts)
Rows 1 and 2: *K1, p1; rep from *
    to end.
Rows 3 and 4: *P1, k1; rep from *
    to end.
Repeat Rows 1–4 for pattern.

Notes

◎ Knit the first and last stitch of every row for selvedge stitches.
◎ Work increases and decreases knitwise or purlwise as necessary to maintain established moss stitch or rib pattern.
◎ Work all increases and decreases on the right side of the work.
◎ The right side and wrong side of the fabric are identical; after working a few rows of ribbing, attach a safety pin to one side of the piece to help keep track of which is the RS.

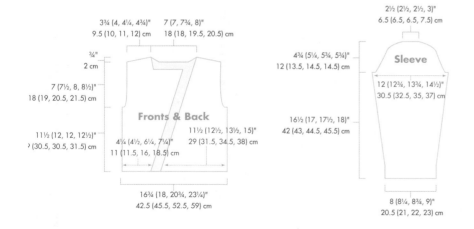

3¾ (4, 4¼, 4¾)"
9.5 (10, 11, 12) cm

7 (7, 7¾, 8)"
18 (18, 19.5, 20.5) cm

¾"
2 cm

7 (7½, 8, 8½)"
18 (19, 20.5, 21.5) cm

Fronts & Back

11½ (12, 12, 12½)"
? (30.5, 30.5, 31.5) cm

4¼ (4½, 6¼, 7¼)"
11 (11.5, 16, 18.5) cm

11½ (12½, 13½, 15)"
29 (31.5, 34.5, 38) cm

16¾ (18, 20¾, 23¼)"
42.5 (45.5, 52.5, 59) cm

2½ (2½, 2½, 3)"
6.5 (6.5, 6.5, 7.5) cm

4¾ (5¼, 5¾, 5¾)"
12 (13.5, 14.5, 14.5) cm

Sleeve

12 (12¾, 13¾, 14½)"
30.5 (32.5, 35, 37) cm

16½ (17, 17½, 18)"
42 (43, 44.5, 45.5) cm

8 (8¼, 8¾, 9)"
20.5 (21, 22, 23) cm

Back

CO 92 (100, 114, 128) sts. Knitting the first and last st of every row, work center 90 (98, 112, 126) sts in k1, p1 rib until piece measures 1½" (3.8 cm) from CO, ending with a WS row. Maintaining selvedge sts as established, work in moss st (see Stitch Guide) until piece measures 11½ (12, 12, 12½)" (29 [30.5, 30.5, 31.5] cm) from CO, ending with a WS row.

SHAPE ARMHOLES | BO 5 (5, 6, 7) sts at beg of next 2 rows, then dec 1 st each end of needle every RS row 2 (4, 6, 9) times—78 (82, 90, 96) sts rem. Cont in patt until armholes measure 7 (7½, 8, 8½)" (18 [19, 20.5, 21.5] cm), ending with a WS row.

SHAPE NECK AND SHOULDERS | Keeping in patt, work 22 (24, 26, 28) sts, join a second ball of yarn and BO center 34 (34, 38, 40) sts, work to end—22 (24, 26, 28) sts rem each side. *Note:* The neck and shoulders are shaped at the same time; read all the way through the foll section before proceeding. Working each side separately, at each armhole edge, BO 5 (6, 6, 7) sts once, then BO 5 (5, 6, 6) sts 2 times and *at the same time,* at each neck edge, dec 1 st every RS row 2 times—5 (6, 6, 7) sts rem when all decs have been completed. BO all sts.

Right Front

CO 23 (25, 34, 40) sts. *Note:* The center front, armhole, and neck are all shaped at the same time; read all the way through the foll sections before proceeding. Knitting the first and last st of every row, work center 21 (23, 32, 38) sts in k1, p1 rib until piece measures 1½" (3.8 cm) from CO, then change to moss st and *at the same time* inc 1 st at beg of every 4th row 32 (34, 34, 36) times as foll: (RS) k1, M1R (see Glossary), work in patt to end. Cont in patt and work incs at center front as established until piece measures 11½ (12, 12, 12½)" (29 [30.5, 30.5, 31.5] cm) from CO, ending with a WS row.

SHAPE ARMHOLE | Cont in patt and working incs at center front as established, at armhole edge (beg of WS rows), BO 5 (5, 6, 7) sts once, then dec 1 st every RS row 2 (4, 6, 9) times—7 (9, 12, 16) sts dec'd at armhole edge. Cont in patt until armhole measures 4½ (5, 5, 5½)" (11.5 [12.5, 12.5, 14] cm), ending with a WS row—48 (50, 56, 60) sts rem after all incs and decs have been completed.

SHAPE NECK AND SHOULDER | With RS facing, BO 24 (24, 28, 30) sts, work to end in patt—24 (26, 28, 30) sts rem. Dec 1 st at neck edge (work as k1, ssk) every 4th row 4 times and *at the same time,* when armhole measures 7 (7½, 8, 8½)" (18 [19, 20.5, 21.5] cm), at armhole edge BO 5 (6, 6, 7) sts once, then BO 5 (5, 6, 6) sts 2 times—5 (6, 6, 7) sts rem. BO all sts.

Left Front

CO 63 (69, 74, 82) sts. *Note:* The center front, armhole, and neck are shaped at the same time; read all the way through the foll sections before proceeding. Knitting the first and last st of every row, work center 61 (67, 72, 80) sts in k1, p1 rib until piece measures 1½" (3.8 cm) from CO, then change to moss st and *at the same time* dec 1 st at the end of every 4th row 36 (38, 38, 40) times as foll: (RS) work to last 3 sts, k2tog, k1. Cont in patt until piece measures 11½ (12, 12, 12½)" (29 [30.5, 30.5, 31.5] cm) from CO, ending with a WS row.

SHAPE ARMHOLE | Cont in patt and work decs at center front as established, at armhole edge (beg of RS rows), BO 5 (5, 6, 7) sts once, then dec 1 st every RS row 2 (4, 6, 9) times—7 (9, 12, 16) sts dec'd at armhole edge. Cont in patt until armhole measures 7 (7½, 8, 8½)" (18 [19, 20.5, 21.5] cm), ending with a WS row—20 (22, 24, 26) sts rem after all incs and decs have been completed.

SHAPE SHOULDER | Keeping in patt, at armhole edge (beg of RS rows), BO 5 (6, 6, 7) sts once, then BO 5 (5, 6, 6) sts 2 times—5 (6, 6, 7) sts rem. BO all sts.

Sleeves (make 2)

CO 44 (46, 48, 50) sts. Knitting the first and last st of every row, work center 42 (44, 46, 48) sts in k1, p1 rib until piece measures 1½" (3.8 cm) from CO, ending with a WS row. Maintaining edge sts as established, change to moss st and work even for 10 rows, ending with a WS row. Inc row: (RS) K1, M1R, work in patt to last st, M1L (see Glossary), k1—2 sts inc'd. Work 9 rows even in patt. Rep the shaping of the last 10 rows 2 (2, 1, 0) more time(s). Next row: (RS) Work inc row, then work 7 rows even in pattern. Rep the shaping of the last 8 rows 7 (8, 11, 13) more times—66 (70, 76, 80) sts. Work even until piece measures 16½ (17, 17½, 18)" (42 [43, 44.5, 45.5] cm) from CO, ending with a WS row.

SHAPE CAP | Keeping in patt, BO 5 (5, 6, 7) sts at beg of next 2 rows—56 (60, 64, 66) sts rem. Dec row: (RS) K1, ssk, work to last 3 sts, k2tog, k1—2 sts dec'd. Work 1 (WS) row even. Dec 1 st each end of needle in this manner every RS row 14 (16, 18, 18) more times—26 (26, 26, 28) sts rem. BO 2 sts at beg of next 6 rows—14 (14, 14, 16) sts rem. BO all sts.

Finishing

Block pieces to measurements. With yarn threaded on a tapestry needle, sew fronts to back at shoulders.

BUTTONHOLE BAND | With RS facing and beg at lower right front, pick up and knit 122 (128, 128, 134) sts evenly spaced along right front edge. Work in k1, p1 rib for 3 rows. Next row: (RS) P2tog, work 3 sts in rib, *BO 3 sts, work 14 (15, 15, 16) sts in rib; rep from * 5 more times, BO 3 sts, work to last st, M1, p1—7 buttonholes made. Next row: Work across all sts, using the backward-loop method (see Glossary) to CO 3 sts over gaps formed by BO sts on

previous row. Work 2 rows even. Next row: K2tog, work to last st, M1, p1. BO all sts in rib patt.

NECK AND BUTTON BAND | With RS facing, pick up and knit 7 sts along top of buttonhole band, 21 (24, 26, 30) sts across BO sts of front neck, 20 (20, 22, 22) sts along front neck edge, 34 (34, 38, 40) sts across BO sts of back neck, 4 sts to shoulder seam, and 136 (141, 143, 159) sts along left front edge—222 (230, 240, 262) sts total. Work in k1, p1 rib for 3 rows. Next row: (RS) Work 2 sts, BO 3 sts, k1, M1, work to last st, M1, p1. Next row: Work in patt, CO 3 sts over gap formed by BO sts on previous row. Keeping in rib patt as established, work short-rows (see Glossary) to raise the back neck as foll:

Row 1: Work 95 (99, 107, 113) sts, wrap next st, turn.
Row 2: Work 52 (52, 56, 58) sts, wrap next st, turn.
Row 3: Work 40 (40, 44, 46) sts, wrap next st, turn.
Row 4: Work 28 (28, 32, 34) sts, wrap next st, turn.
Row 5: Work to end of row.
Row 6: Work across all sts, working the wraps tog with the wrapped sts.
Row 7: Work 7 sts, M1, work to last st, M1, p1.
Next row: BO all sts in rib.
With yarn threaded on a tapestry needle, sew sleeve caps into armholes. Sew sleeve and side seams. Weave in loose ends.
Sew buttons to button band, opposite buttonholes.

Shine

By now you may have worked through some of the previous projects in this book, or maybe you're already a fan of fine yarns and are itching for a challenge. Fine yarns present almost unlimited creative possibilities. This section is full of projects that will help you break into innovative techniques and more complex skills. We'll walk you through them, and in the end, you'll have no reason (or desire) to shy away from any type of project knitted in skinny yarn.

Projects

Bohus-Inspired Pullover

Travelling Stitch Legwarmers

Lattice Lace Pullover

Zip-Front Hoodie

Lace Stole

Fingerless Elbow Gloves

Bohus-Inspired Pullover

CAROL SULCOSKI

Inspired by the beautiful sweaters of the Swedish Bohus tradition, this yoked pullover is knitted in a laceweight wool/silk-blend yarn that is double-stranded throughout for quicker knitting and greater color interest. The soft heathery color gradations in the yoke are achieved by changing the color of one strand at a time according to a regular stripe sequence. The sweater is worked in the round from the hem to the yoke; a bit of lace decorates the three-quarter-length sleeves.

Finished Size 32 (36, 40, 44, 48)" (81.5 [91.5, 101.5, 112, 122] cm) bust circumference. Sweater shown measures 32" (81.5 cm).

Yarn Laceweight (#0 Lace).
Shown here: Jaggerspun Zephyr (50% merino wool, 50% tussah silk; 630 yd [576 m]/2 oz): ice blue (MC) 3 (4, 4, 4, 5) balls; marine blue (CC1), Aegean blue (CC2), juniper (CC3), peacock (CC4), jade (CC5), and teal (CC6), 1 ball each.

Needles Body and sleeves—U.S. size 4 (3.5 mm): 24" (60 cm) circular (cir) and set of 4 or 5 double-pointed (dpn). Edging— U.S. size 3 (3 mm): 24" (60 cm) cir and set of 4 or 5 dpn. Adjust needle size if necessary to obtain the correct gauge.

Notions Markers (m); stitch holders or waste yarn; tapestry needle.

Gauge 28 stitches and 40 rounds = 4" (10 cm) in stockinette stitch worked in the round on larger needles with 2 strands of yarn.

Notes

◎ The yarn is used double-stranded throughout. The body of the garment is worked with two strands of the main color held together. For the yoke, colors progress from dark blue to pale green by changing the color of the yarn one strand at a time.

◎ If you'd prefer a higher neckline, simply continue in the last color combination (2 strands of CC6) until the neckline is the desired height.

◎ If you'd like to use your own colorway but are feeling tentative about which ones work well together, try selecting a primary or primary-based color for the main color and a secondary color that contains that primary color for use in the yoke. For example, the sample sweater uses a shade of blue, a primary color, for the main color and shades of green (a mixture of blue and yellow) and blue for the contrasting colors. Another example is to use marigold (a shade of the primary color yellow) as the main color and shades of orange (a mixture of yellow and red) and yellow for the contrasting colors.

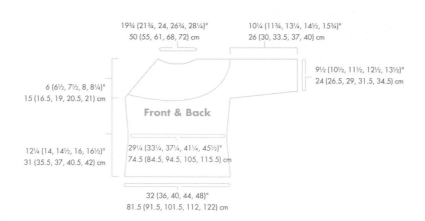

19¾ (21¾, 24, 26¾, 28¼)"
50 (55, 61, 68, 72) cm

10¼ (11¾, 13¼, 14½, 15¾)"
26 (30, 33.5, 37, 40) cm

9½ (10½, 11½, 12½, 13½)"
24 (26.5, 29, 31.5, 34.5) cm

6 (6½, 7½, 8, 8¼)"
15 (16.5, 19, 20.5, 21) cm

Front & Back

12¼ (14, 14½, 16, 16½)"
31 (35.5, 37, 40.5, 42) cm

29¼ (33¼, 37¼, 41¼, 45½)"
74.5 (84.5, 94.5, 105, 115.5) cm

32 (36, 40, 44, 48)"
81.5 (91.5, 101.5, 112, 122) cm

Stitch Guide

Yoke Color Pattern

Work 5 (6, 6, 7, 7) rounds of each of the following color combinations.

2 strands CC1.

1 strand each of CC1 and CC2.

2 strands CC2.

1 strand each of CC2 and CC3.

2 strands CC3.

1 strand each of CC3 and CC4.

2 strands CC4.

1 strand each of CC4 and CC5.

2 strands CC5.

1 strand each of CC5 and CC6.

2 strands CC6.

LACE BAND

Symbol	Meaning
•	p
☐	k
╱	k2tog
○	yo
╲	ssk
𝝺	sl 1, k2tog, psso

Body

With smaller cir needle and 2 strands of MC held tog, CO 112 (126, 140, 154, 168) sts, place marker (pm) to mark side seam, then CO 112 (126, 140, 154, 168) sts—224 (252, 280, 308, 336) total. Pm to mark beg of rnd and join for working in rnds, being careful not to twist sts. Work in St st (knit all rnds) until piece measures 1" (2.5 cm) from CO (for facing). Change to larger cir needle and purl 1 rnd for turning ridge. Cont in St st until piece measures 1¼ (2, 2¼, 3, 3¼)" (3.2 [5, 5.5, 7.5, 8.5] cm) from turning ridge. **Dec rnd:** K2, k2tog, knit to 4 sts before side m, ssk, k2, slip marker (sl m), k2, k2tog, knit to last 4 sts, ssk, k2—4 sts dec'd. Knit 14 rnds even. Rep the last 15 rnds 2 more times—212 (240, 268, 296, 324) sts rem. Rep dec rnd. Knit 9 rnds even. Rep dec rnd—204 (232, 260, 288, 316) sts rem. **Inc rnd:** K2, M1R (see Glossary), knit to 2 sts before side m, M1L (see Glossary), k2, sl m, k2, M1R, knit to last 2 sts, M1L, k2—4 sts inc'd. Knit 9 rnds even. Rep the last 10 rnds once more—212 (240, 268, 296, 324) sts. Rep inc rnd. Knit 14 rnds. Rep the last 15 rnds 2 more times—224 (252, 280, 308, 336) sts. Cont even until

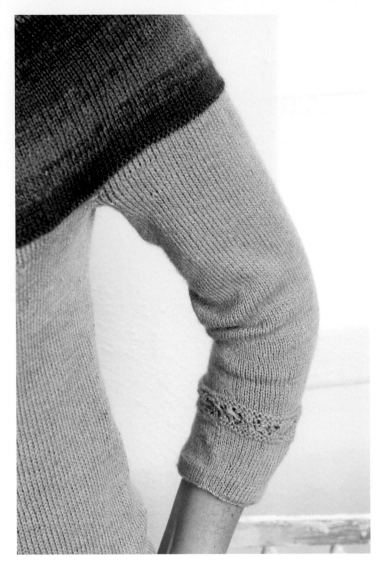

piece measures 12¼ (14, 14½, 16, 16½)" (31 [35.5, 37, 40.5, 42] cm) from turning ridge. **Next rnd:** Knit to 5 (7, 7, 7, 10) sts before side m, BO 10 (14, 14, 14, 20) sts (remove marker), knit to 5 (7, 7, 7, 10) sts before end of rnd m, BO 10 (14, 14, 14, 20) sts—102 (112, 126, 140, 148) sts rem each for front and back. Set aside.

Sleeves (make 2)

With smaller dpn and 2 strands of MC, CO 67 (74, 81, 88, 95) sts. Pm and join for working in rnds, being careful not to twist sts. Knit 10 rnds. Change to larger needles and purl 1 rnd for turning ridge. Knit 11 rnds. **Next rnd:** K2, M1L, knit to last 4 sts, M1R, k2, M1R, knit to end—70 (77, 84, 91, 98) sts. Knit 10 rnds. Work Rows 1–11 of Lace Band chart. **Next rnd:** Knit, inc 0 (0, 0, 1, 0) st—70 (77, 84, 92, 98) sts.

Sizes 32", 40", 44", and 48" only Next rnd: K2, M1L, k2, M1L, knit to last 4 sts, M1R, k2, M1R, knit to end—4 sts inc'd.

Size 36" only Next rnd: K2, M1L, knit to last 4 sts, M1R, k2, M1R, knit to end—3 sts inc'd.

All sizes Knit 7 rnds. Inc rnd: K2, M1L, knit to last 2 sts, M1R, k2—2 sts inc'd. Rep the last 8 rnds 3 (5, 5, 6, 6) more times—82 (92, 100, 110, 116) sts.

Size 48" only Knit 4 rnds. Inc rnd: K2, M1L, k2, M1L, knit to last 4 sts, M1R, k2, M1R, knit to end—4 sts inc'd.

All sizes After all shaping is complete, there will be 82 (92, 100, 110, 120) sts. Cont even until piece measures 10¼ (11¾, 13¼, 14½, 15¾)" (26 [30, 33.5, 37, 40] cm) from turning ridge. **Next rnd:** Knit to last 5 (7, 7, 7, 10) sts, BO 10 (14, 14, 14, 20) sts, work to end—72 (78, 86, 96, 100) sts rem. Set aside.

Yoke

With 2 strands of MC and larger cir needle, join pieces as foll: k72 (78, 86, 96, 100) sts from one sleeve, pm, k102 (112, 126, 140, 148) front sts, pm, k72 (78, 86, 96, 100) sts from other sleeve, pm, k102 (112, 126, 140, 148) back sts, pm—348 (380, 424, 472, 496) sts total. Knit 1 rnd, dec 3 (0, 0, 4, 2, 1) st(s) near armholes where they will be less noticeable—345 (380,

420, 470, 495) sts rem. Change to 2 strands of CC1 and knit 1 rnd, then purl 1 rnd. Work the 5 (6, 6, 7, 7) rnds of each color combination as specified in the Stitch Guide and *at the same time* shape the yoke as foll: Work even until yoke measures 2 (2, 2¼, 2½, 2½)" (5 [5, 5.5, 6.5, 6.5] cm) from purl ridge. **Next rnd:** *K3, k2tog; rep from *—276 (304, 336, 376, 396) sts rem. Work even until yoke measures 4 (4, 4½, 5, 5)" (10 [10, 11.5, 12.5, 12.5] cm) from purl ridge. **Next rnd:** *K2, k2tog; rep from *— 207 (228, 252, 282, 297) sts rem. Work even until yoke measures 5¾ (6, 6¾, 7¼, 7½)" (14.5 [15, 17, 18.5, 19] cm)

from purl ridge. **Next rnd:** *K1, k2tog; rep from *—138 (152, 168, 188, 198) sts rem for neck. Cont even in color patt until there are at least 8 rnds worked with 2 strands of CC6. Purl 1 rnd for turning ridge. Change to smaller cir needle and knit 6 rnds for facing. BO alls sts.

Finishing

Block to measurements. Turn facings to WS along purl ridges and with yarn threaded on a tapestry needle, sew in place. Sew underarm seams. Weave in loose ends.

Traveling Stitch Legwarmers

LISA R. MYERS

These legwarmers more closely resemble close-fitting leggings than the slouchy legwarmers of the 1980s. They hug the leg from the cuff to the thigh in an elaborate traveling-stitch pattern that comes from traditional Austrian knee socks. The calves are shaped with increases and decreases hidden in a lozenge-shaped motif. Warmer and more comfortable than tights, you'll want to pull these on with your favorite skirt all winter long.

Finished Size About 10" (25.5 cm) circumference at widest part and 22½" (57 cm) long. To fit a woman.

Yarn Sportweight (#2 Fine). *Shown here:* Brown Sheep Nature Spun Sport (100% wool; 184 yd [168 m]/50 g): #117S winter blue, 3 balls.

Needles U.S. size 3 (3.25 mm): set of 4 or 5 double-pointed (dpn). Adjust needle size if necessary to obtain the correct gauge.

Notions Markers (m); cable needle (cn); tapestry needle.

Gauge 37 stitches and 42 rows = 4" (10 cm) in reverse stockinette stitch.

Stitch Guide

Twisted Rib (multiple of 2 sts)
Rnd 1: *K1 through back loop (tbl), p1; rep from * to end of rnd.
Repeat this round for pattern.

Legwarmer (make 2)

CO 58 sts. Divide sts as evenly as possible on 3 or 4 dpn, place marker (pm), and join for working in rnds, being careful not to twist sts. Work twisted rib (see Stitch Guide) for 10 rnds. **Set-up rnd:** P11, pm, work set-up rnd of Double Twist chart over next 12 sts for front of leg, pm, p21, pm, work set-up rnd of Open Twist chart over next 4 sts for back of leg, pm, p10 to end of rnd. Work in patt as established for 34 more rnds, ending with Rnd 4 of Double Twist chart and Rnd 4 of Open Twist chart—piece measures about 5" (12.5 cm) from CO. Cont Double Twist chart as established, but work Rnds 1–98 of Lozenge chart over 4 sts that had been worked according to Open Twist chart—62 sts; piece measures about 14" (35.5 cm) from CO. The 8 sts rem from the Lozenge chart will look very similar to Rnd 3 of the Double Twist chart, which is the rnd you are about to work on the front of the leg. Move the rnd marker exactly halfway around (31 sts each side of marker) and count the beg of the rnd from that point. *Note:* If, by some chance, you're on a different round at the front of the leg, don't worry—you'll just have to keep track of the patterns separately; no one will notice if they're not perfectly aligned. Work 6 rnds even in patt, working Double Twist chart as established on front of leg and working Double Twist chart above the Lozenge chart on the back of the leg. **Inc rnd:** Inc 1 st purlwise just before and just after the pattern panel at the back of the leg—2 sts inc'd. Work 3 rnds even. Rep the last 4 rows 7 more times, ending with Rnd 10 of Double Twist chart—piece measures 19½" (49.5 cm) from CO, 78 sts. Work Rnd 1 of Double Twist chart once more, then work twisted rib for 3" (7.5 cm). BO all sts in k1, p1 rib (untwisted).

Finishing

Weave in loose ends. Block lightly if desired.

OPEN TWIST

DOUBLE TWIST

Legend

ℓ	k1tbl
•	purl
⟍⟋ b b	sl 1 st onto cn and hold in back, k1tbl, then k1tbl from cn
⟍⟋ b	sl 1 st onto cn and hold in back, k1tbl, then p1 from cn
⟋⟍ b b	sl 1 st onto cn and hold in front, k1tbl, then k1tbl from cn
⟍⟋ b	sl 1 st onto cn and hold in back, k1tbl, then p1 from cn
⟋⟍ b	sl 1 st onto cn and hold in front, p1, then k1tbl from cn
☐	pattern repeat

LOZENGE, RNDS 39–98

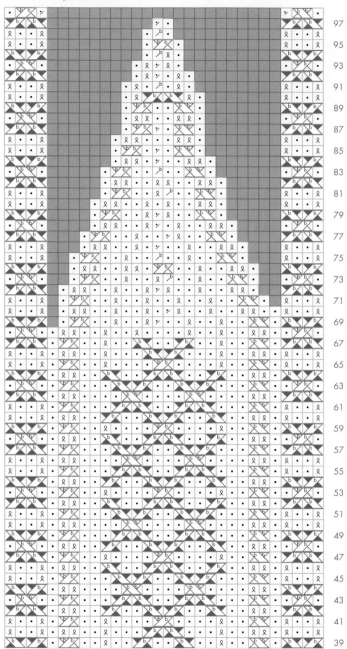

97
95
93
91
89
87
85
83
81
79
77
75
73
71
69
67
65
63
61
59
57
55
53
51
49
47
45
43
41
39

໐	k1tbl on RS, p1tbl on WS		no stitch
	k on RS; p on WS		k2tog tbl
•	p on RS; k on WS	M	M1
	p2tog	MP	M1 pwise

sl 1 st onto cn and hold in back, then k1 tbl, k1tbl from cn

sl 1 st onto cn and hold in front, then k1 tbl, k1tbl from cn

sl 1 st onto cn and hold in back, then k1tbl, p1 from cn

sl 1 st onto cn and hold in front, then p1, k1tbl from cn

LOZENGE, RNDS 1–38

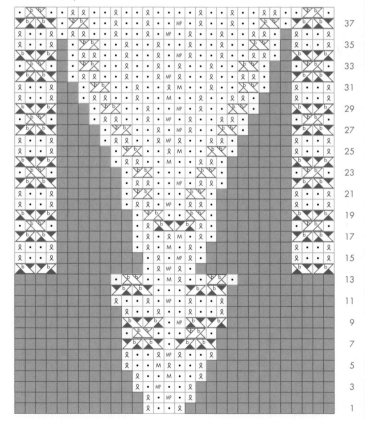

37
35
33
31
29
27
25
23
21
19
17
15
13
11
9
7
5
3
1

Traveling Stitch Tips

The traveling stitch patterns in this project are really just cable patterns on an extremely small scale: One stitch crosses over another. (Plus the added difference that the knit stitches are worked through the back of the loop, to twist them and bring the design into higher relief.) So you can work them as you would any cable, with whatever cable needle you like or with none at all. But with so few stitches involved, you have a couple more options to speed the process up:

◎ Work the stitches out of order. Insert the point of the right-hand needle into the second stitch on the left-hand needle; wrap the yarn around and pull the new stitch through, but without letting the old stitch fall off the left needle; insert the right needle into the first stitch and work it as usual; release both old stitches from the left needle together. That will twist the second stitch in front of the first. If the second stitch needs to go behind the first, bring the point of the right needle behind the work and insert it through the back of the loop of the second stitch, then proceed as above.

◎ Cheat. Okay, we're sure we're not supposed to call it that because this is an authentic traditional method, but it feels like a modern convenience: Insert the point of the right-hand needle into both stitches as if to knit two together; wrap the yarn and pull the new stitch through but without letting the old stitches fall off the needle; insert the right needle into just the first stitch and knit it a second time; release both old stitches from the left needle.

Each of these methods presents its own set of challenges for some crossings (especially the case where the first stitch is knit and the second is to be purled), but you may find that they are still more efficient than stopping to pick up a cable needle every time.

Lattice Lace | Pullover

LAURA GRUTZECK

This highly textured pullover makes the most of a lightweight springy wool yarn. The stitch pattern is a lace motif composed of simple yarnovers and decreases, but the springy nature of the yarn gives the impression of twisted cables as well. Because the stitch count changes from row to row, the armhole and neck shaping are a little tricky, but you'll be rewarded with a comfortable sweater with wear-everywhere appeal.

Finished Size 36 (38, 42, 48)" (91.5 [96.5, 106.5, 122] cm) bust circumference. Sweater shown measures 38" (96.5 cm).

Yarn Fingering weight (#1 Super Fine). *Shown here:* Koigu Premium Merino (100% merino; 170 yd [155 m]/50 g): #2343 sage, 12 (13, 15, 18) skeins.

Needles U.S. size 3 (3.25 mm): 16" and 24" (60 and 80 cm) circular (cir). Adjust needle size if necessary to obtain the correct gauge.

Notions Markers (m); stitch holders; tapestry needle.

Gauge 31½ stitches and 42¾ rows = 4" (10 cm) according to Lattice Lace chart, after light steam-blocking.

Notes

◎ The stitch count changes during the 12-row charted pattern; check your stitch count after Rows 5, 6, 11, or 12; the other rows will have a different number of stitches per repeat.

◎ This lace pattern has a lot of stretch and the weight of the sweater will add vertical length. For this reason, some of the measurements are given with the piece hanging, not laid flat.

◎ Because the lace pattern stretches in width as well as length, the finished measurement will easily accommodate a bust of the same size and still provide suitable ease.

◎ The first and last stitch of every row are selvedge stitches (they are not part of the lattice pattern); they should be knitted every row.

◎ When decreasing for the armhole and sleeve caps and increasing for the sleeve, stitch markers are used to keep track of pattern repeats. Each time the markers are moved, re-establish the lace pattern by working the entire chart between markers, including the stitches before and after the repeat box.

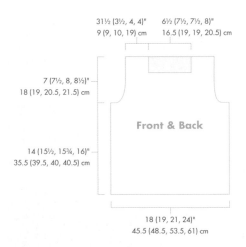

31½ (3½, 4, 4)"
9 (9, 10, 19) cm

6½ (7½, 7½, 8)"
16.5 (19, 19, 20.5) cm

7 (7½, 8, 8½)"
18 (19, 20.5, 21.5) cm

Front & Back

14 (15½, 15¾, 16)"
35.5 (39.5, 40, 40.5) cm

18 (19, 21, 24)"
45.5 (48.5, 53.5, 61) cm

2½ (2½, 2½, 3)"
6.5 (6.5, 6.5, 7.5) cm

3½ (3¾, 4¼, 4½)"
9 (9.5, 11, 11.5) cm

11½ (12½, 13½, 14½)"
29 (31.5, 34.5, 37) cm

Sleeve

16½ (17, 17, 17½)"
42 (43, 43, 44.5) cm

7½ (8½, 9½, 10½)"
19 (21.5, 24, 26.5) cm

LATTICE LACE

☐	k on RS; p on WS
╱	k2tog
○	yo
╲	ssk
▨	no stitch
▢	pattern repeat

Back

With longer needle, CO 141 (149, 165, 189) sts. Do not join. Knit 1 (WS) row. **Set-up row:** (RS) K1 (selvedge st; knit every row), work Row 1 of Lattice Lace chart across 139 (147, 163, 187) sts, k1 (selvedge st; knit every row). Cont as established, work Rows 2–12 of chart once, then rep Rows 1–12 until piece measures 14 (15½, 15¾, 16)" (35.5 [39.5, 40, 40.5] cm) from CO, ending with Row 5 of patt.

SHAPE ARMHOLES | BO 8 sts at beg of next 2 rows—1 full lace rep dec'd at each armhole edge. **Next row:** (WS; Row 8 of chart) K1, p7, place marker (pm), purl to last 8 sts, pm, p7, k1. Re-establish patt and dec at each armhole edge on next 3 RS rows as foll:

Dec Row 1: (RS) K1, [k2tog] 3 times, k1, slip marker (sl m), work in patt to next m, sl m, k1, [ssk] 3 times, k1—6 sts dec'd.

Dec Row 2: (RS) K1, [k2tog] 2 times, sl m, work in patt to next m, sl m, [ssk] 2 times, k1—4 sts dec'd.

Dec Row 3: (RS) K1, k2tog, sl m, work in patt to next m, sl m, ssk, k1—2 sts dec'd 111 (119, 135, 159) sts rem after Rows 5, 6, 11, and 12 of chart (98 [105, 119, 140] sts rem after other rows of chart). Remove markers on next row and cont as directed below for your size.

Sizes 36" and 38" only Re-establish patt and dec as foll. Next RS row: K1, pm, start first patt rep of Row 3 as k3tog instead of k2tog, work in patt to last 3 sts, ssk, pm, k1—2 sts dec'd. Skip to All Sizes below.

Sizes 42" and 48" only Next WS row: Reposition markers as foll. K1, p8, pm, purl to last 9 sts, p8, k1. Re-establish patt and dec as foll. Next row: (RS) K1, [k2tog] 3 times, knit to m, sl m, work in patt to next m, sl m, k2, [ssk] 3 times, k1—6 sts dec'd. Work 1 (WS) row even. Next row: (RS) K1, [k2tog] 2 times, k1, sl m, work in patt to next m, sl m, k1, [ssk] 2 times, k1—4 sts dec'd. Work 1 (WS) row even. Next row: (RS) K1, k2tog, k1, sl m, work in patt to next m, k1, ssk, k1—2 sts dec'd. Skip to All Sizes below.

Size 48" only Next WS row: Reposition markers as foll. K1, p9, pm, purl to last 10 sts, p9, k1. Re-establish patt and dec as foll. Next row: (RS) K1, [k2tog] 3 times, knit to m, sl m, work in patt to next m, sl m, k3, [ssk] 3 times, k—6 sts dec'd. Work 1 (WS) row even. Next row: (RS) K1, [k2tog] 2 times, k2, sl m, work in patt to next m, sl m, k2, [ssk] 2 times, k1—4 sts dec'd. Work 1 (WS) row even. Next row: (RS) K1, k2tog, k2, sl m, work in patt to next m, k2, ssk, k1—2 sts dec'd.

All sizes From this point on there will be 109 (117, 121, 131) sts after working Rows 5, 6, 11, and 12 of chart. Cont even in patt until armholes measure about 7 (7½, 8, 8½)" (18 [19, 20.5, 21.5] cm) when hanging (not laid flat; see Notes), ending with Row 11 of chart.

Front

CO and work as for back until armholes measure about 1¼" (3.2 cm) shorter than for back, ending with Row 11 of chart.

SHAPE NECK | (WS; Row 12 of chart) K1 (selvedge st; knit every row), p27 (27, 29, 30) for left front, k1 (selvedge st; knit every row), place rem sts on holders as foll: 51 (59, 59, 67) sts on one holder for center front neck; 29 (29, 31, 32) sts on another holder for right front. Cont working patt as established, including the sts before and after the patt rep box (*Note:* For sizes 42 and 48, the patt will be worked between the first selvedge st and the marker at left edge) for 11 more rows, ending with Row 11 of chart. Place sts on holder. Place 29 (29, 31, 32) sts for right front on needles, rejoin yarn, and beg with Row 12 of patt, work 12 rows total. Place sts on holder.

Sleeves (make 2)

With longer needle, CO 61 (69, 77, 85) sts. Do not join. **Next row:** (WS) K1 (selvedge st; knit every row), pm, knit to last st, pm, k1 (selvedge st; knit every row). Keeping the selvedge sts in garter st, work center 59 (67, 75, 83) sts according to Rows 1–12 of Lattice Lace chart. **Next row:** (RS) K1, yo, sl m, work Row 1 of chart to m, sl m, yo, k1—2 sts inc'd. Inc 1 st each end of needle in this manner every 10th row 6 more times. The first set of increases will fall on Rows 1, 11, 9, 7, 5, 3, and 1 of chart. Re-establish patt and cont to inc as foll: **Next row:** (WS; Row 2 of chart) Remove markers. **Next row:** (Row 3 of chart) K1, pm, work Row 3 to last st, pm, k1. Inc every 10th row 6 more times. The second set of increases will fall on Rows 11, 9, 7, 5, 3, 1, and 11 of chart. Work 2 rows even (Rows 12 and 1 of chart). Re-establish patt and cont to inc as foll. **Next row:** (WS; Row 2 of chart) Remove markers. **Next row:** (Row 3 of chart) K1, pm, work Row 3 to last st, pm, k1—93 (101, 109, 117) sts after Rows 5, 6, 11, and 12 of chart. Cont even in patt until piece measures about 16½ (17, 17, 17½)" (42 [43, 43, 44.5] cm) when hanging (not laid flat), ending with Row 11 of chart.

SHAPE CAP | BO 8 sts at beg of next 2 rows—1 full lace rep dec'd at each armhole edge. Re-establish patt and dec as foll. **Next row:** (Row 2 of chart) K1, p7, pm, purl to last 8 sts, pm, p7, k1. (*Note:* As you work the cap shaping, there will be fewer and fewer sts outside the markers. When there aren't enough sts left before and after the markers to complete a decrease, move another group of 7 or 8 sts to the outside of the marker; move 7 sts to the decrease side of marker after working Row 1, 3, 7, or 9 of patt; move 8 sts after working Row 5 or 11. There should always be full pattern repeats between the markers, including the beginning and ending repeats on the chart.) Dec 1 st each end of needle every RS row 12 (12, 14, 15) times as foll. **Dec Row:** (RS) Knit to 2 sts before first m, k2tog, sl m, work in patt to next m, sl m, ssk, knit to end—2 sts dec'd. Work 1 WS row even. Dec 2 sts each end of needle every RS row 6 (7, 8, 9) times as foll: **Double Dec Row:** (RS) K1, k2tog, knit to 2 sts before m, ssk, sl m, work in patt to next m, sl m, k2tog, knit to last 3 sts, ssk, k1—4 sts dec'd. Work 1 (WS) row even—21 (25, 25, 27) sts rem after all cap shaping is complete, when counted after Rows 5, 6, 11, and 12 of patt. BO all sts.

Finishing

With RS facing tog and using the three-needle method (see Glossary), BO 29 (29, 31, 32) sts for each front shoulder to the corresponding 29 (29, 31, 32) sts for each back shoulder.

NECK | Place 51 (59, 59, 67) held back neck sts on one needle. With shorter cir needle and RS facing, join yarn to left side of sts and pick up and knit 16 sts along side of neck, k51 (59, 59, 67) held front neck sts, pick up and knit 13 sts along other side of neck, k51 (59, 59, 67) back neck sts—131 (147, 147, 163) sts total. Join for working in rnds, but do not place marker yet. K4, pm for beg of rnd. Beg with Rnd 1, work lace patt in rnds (knit all even-numbered rows instead of purling them) until neck measures about 5" (12.5 cm)

from pick-up rnd, ending with an even-numbered patt row. **Next rnd:** Purl all sts. BO all sts purlwise.

Lightly steam-block all pieces with WS facing up, being careful not to stretch the lace patt (which will cause the work to flatten and grow). With yarn threaded on a tapestry needle, sew sleeve caps into armholes. Sew sleeve and side seams. Weave in loose ends.

Zip-Front Hoodie

LISA R. MYERS

Fitted and feminine, this lightly cabled hoodie is comfortable without being sloppy. The body is worked in one piece from the lower edge to the armhole, with waist shaping hidden in the cable pattern for a streamlined seamless look, then the fronts and back (and sleeves) are worked separately to the shoulders. The cotton/silk-blend yarn is equally welcome at the beach on summer evenings and indoors on cool winter days.

Finished Size 32 (36, 40, 44, 48)" (81.5 [91.5, 101.5, 112, 122] cm) bust circumference, zipped. Sweater shown measures 40" (101.5 cm).

Yarn Sportweight (#2 Fine).
Shown here: Zitron Kokon (35% silk, 35% cotton, 30% acrylic; [175 m]/50 g): #22 light blue, 8 (9, 9, 10, 10) balls.

Needles U.S. size 4 (3.5 mm): 24" (60 cm) circular (cir). Adjust needle size if necessary to obtain the correct gauge.

Notions Cable needle (cn); stitch holders; tapestry needle; 22" (56 cm) separating zipper; sharp-point sewing needle; contrasting thread for basting zipper; matching thread for securing zipper.

Gauge 24 stitches and 36 rows = 4" (10 cm) in stockinette stitch; 16-stitch cable panel measures 2" (5 cm) wide.

Stitch Guide

**Cable Decrease
(worked over 18 sts)**
Sl 1 st purlwise, slip next 2 sts onto cn and hold in back of work, return single sl st to left-hand needle, k2tog, k1, k2 from cn, k8, sl next 2 sts to cn and hold in front, k2, k1 from cn, sl second st from cn, k1, psso—2 sts dec'd.

**Cable Increase
(worked over 16 sts)**
Sl next 2 sts onto cn and hold in back of work, insert tip of right-hand needle under horizontal bar between last knitted st and first st on cn, wrap yarn around needle and pull a new st through, k2, k2 from cn, k8, sl next 2 sts onto cn and hold in front, k2, k2 from cn, insert tip of right-hand needle under horizontal bar between last knitted st and next st, wrap yarn around needle, and pull a new st through—2 sts inc'd.

Notes

◎ The body is worked in a single piece to the armholes, then the fronts and back are worked separately to the shoulders.

◎ The 22" (56 cm) zipper should fit on all sizes. If it does not fit the front of your sweater exactly, ask your local fabric shop about having the zipper custom-shortened.

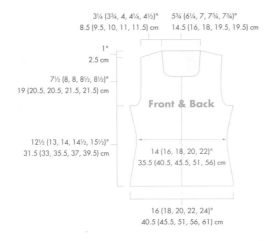

3¼ (3¾, 4, 4¼, 4½)"
8.5 (9.5, 10, 11, 11.5) cm

5¾ (6¼, 7, 7¾, 7¾)"
14.5 (16, 18, 19.5, 19.5) cm

1"
2.5 cm

7½ (8, 8, 8½, 8½)"
19 (20.5, 20.5, 21.5, 21.5) cm

Front & Back

12½ (13, 14, 14½, 15½)"
31.5 (33, 35.5, 37, 39.5) cm

14 (16, 18, 20, 22)"
35.5 (40.5, 45.5, 51, 56) cm

16 (18, 20, 22, 24)"
40.5 (45.5, 51, 56, 61) cm

2¼ (3, 3, 3, 3)"
5.5 (7.5, 7.5, 7.5, 7.5) cm

5½ (5¾, 5¾, 6¼, 6¼)"
14 (14.5, 14.5, 16, 16) cm

Sleeve

15¼ (16, 16, 16¾, 17)"
38.5 (40.5, 40.5, 42.5, 43) cm

17½"
44.5 cm

8 (8, 8¾, 8¾, 8¾)"
20.5 (20.5, 22, 22, 22) cm

Body

CO 200 (228, 248, 276, 296) sts.

Row 1: (RS) Sl 1 (selvedge st), work last 8 sts of Row 1 of Cable chart, [p2, k2] 8 (10, 11, 13, 14) times, p2, work Row 1 of Cable chart over next 16 sts, [p2, k2] 20 (23, 26, 29, 32) times, p2, work Row 1 of Cable chart over next 16 sts, [p2, k2] 8 (10, 11, 13, 14) times, p2, work first 8 sts of Row 1 of Cable chart, sl 1 (selvedge st).

Row 2: P1, work sts as they appear (knit the knits and purl the purls) to last st, p1.

Cont in patt as established (i.e., sl first and last st on every RS row, work cable panel at center front and side "seams," work all other sts in k2, p2 rib) for 7 more rows, ending with a RS row. Inc row: (WS) Purl, inc 2 (0, 2, 0, 2) sts evenly spaced between first and second cable panels (for left front), inc 2 sts between second and third cable panels (for back), and inc 2 (0, 2, 0, 2) sts between third and fourth cable panels (for right front)—206 (230, 254, 278, 302) sts. Cont to work selvedge sts and cable panels as established, work body sts in St st for 6 (6, 6, 12, 12) rows more, ending with a WS row.

SHAPE WAIST | Dec row: (RS) Keeping in patt, work to 1 st before second cable panel (i.e., right underarm), work cable dec (see Stitch Guide), work to next cable panel (i.e., left underarm), rep cable dec, work to end of row—4 sts dec'd. Work 5 rows even. Rep the shaping of the last 6 rows 4 more times, then work dec row once more—182 (206, 230, 254, 278) sts rem. Work 11 rows even. Inc row: (RS) Work to second cable panel, work cable inc (see Stitch Guide), work to next cable panel, rep cable inc, work to end of row—4 sts inc'd. Work 5 rows even. Rep the shaping of the last 6 rows 4 more times, then work inc row once more—206 (230, 254, 278, 302) sts. Cont even until piece measures about 12½ (13, 14, 14½, 15½)" (31.5 (33, 35.5, 37, 39.5] cm) from CO, ending with Row 4 of chart.

DIVIDE FOR FRONT AND BACK | Work to second cable panel, *work cable sts as foll: slip next 2 sts onto cn and hold behind left-hand needle, [k2tog (1 st from each needle)] 2 times, k8, sl next 2 sts onto cn and hold in front of left-hand needle, [k2tog (1 st from each needle)] 2 times, sl 12 rem sts from cable panel to holder**, knit to next cable panel, rep from * to ** once, work to end of row—174 (198, 222, 246, 270) sts rem; 45 (51, 57, 63, 69) sts for each front, 84 (96, 108, 120, 132) sts for back.

LEFT FRONT | Maintaining cable panel and selvedge st at front edge as established, dec 1 st at armhole edge every RS row 4 (2, 5, 10, 16) times, then every 4th row 2 (4, 4, 2, 0) times—39 (45, 48, 51, 53) sts rem. Cont even until armhole measures 4½ (5, 5, 5½, 5½)" (11.5 [12.5, 12.5, 14, 14] cm), ending with a RS row. Make note of which row of cable panel was worked last so you make the right front match.

Shape Neck (WS) P14 (17, 17, 18, 18) sts and place on holder, purl to end of row—25 (28, 31, 33, 35) sts rem. Dec 1 st at neck edge every RS row 4 (4, 4, 5, 5) times, then every other RS row (i.e., every 4th row) 2 (2, 3, 3, 3) times—19 (22, 24, 25, 27) sts rem. Work even until armhole measures 7½ (8, 8, 8½, 8½)" (19 [20.5, 20.5, 21.5, 21.5] cm), ending with a WS row.

Shape Shoulder At armhole edge (beg of RS rows), BO 7 (8, 8, 9, 9) sts 1 (1, 3, 1, 3) time(s), then BO 6 (7, 0, 8, 0) sts 2 (2, 0, 2, 0) times.

CABLE

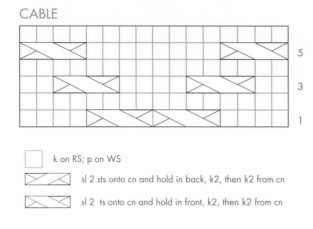

☐ k on RS; p on WS

◸◹ sl 2 sts onto cn and hold in back, k2, then k2 from cn

◺◿ sl 2 ts onto cn and hold in front, k2, then k2 from cn

RIGHT FRONT | Rejoin yarn at armhole edge. Maintaining cable panel and selvedge st at front edge as established, dec 1 st at armhole edge every WS row 4 (2, 5, 10, 16) times, then every 4th row 2 (4, 4, 2, 0) times—39 (45, 48, 51, 53) sts rem. Cont even until armhole measures 4½ (5, 5, 5½, 5½)" (11.5 [12.5, 12.5, 14, 14] cm), ending with a RS row and making sure that the cable ends at the same point as the left front.

Shape Neck (RS) K14 (17, 17, 18, 18) sts and place on holder, knit to end of row—25 (28, 31, 33, 35) sts rem. Dec 1 st at neck edge every RS row 4 (4, 4, 5, 5) times, then every other RS row (i.e., every 4th row) 2 (2, 3, 3, 3) times—19 (22, 24, 25, 27) sts rem. Work even until armhole measures 7½ (8, 8, 8½, 8½)" (19 [20.5, 20.5, 21.5, 21.5] cm), ending with a RS row.

Shape Shoulder At armhole edge (beg of WS rows), BO 7 (8, 8, 9, 9) sts 1 (1, 3, 1, 3) time(s), then BO 6 (7, 0, 8, 0) sts 2 (2, 0, 2, 0) times.

BACK | Rejoin yarn to 84 (96, 108, 120, 132) back sts at left armhole edge. Purl 1 row. Dec 1 st each end of needle every RS row 4 (2, 5, 10, 16) times, then every other RS row (2, 4, 4, 2, 0) times—72 (84, 90, 96, 100) sts rem. Work even until piece measures same as fronts to shoulder.

Shape Shoulders BO 7 (8, 8, 9, 9) sts at beg of next 2 (2, 6, 2, 6) rows, then BO 6 (7, 0, 8, 0) sts at beg of foll 2 (2, 0, 2, 0) rows—46 (54, 42, 62, 46) sts rem. Place sts on holder.

Sleeves (make 2)

CO 48 (48, 52, 52, 52) sts. **Set-up row:** (RS) P1, work last 8 sts of Row 1 of Cable chart, [p2, k2] 7 (7, 8, 8, 8) times, p2, work first 8 sts of Row 1 of Cable chart, p1. Work 8 more rows as established. Maintaining first and last sts in cable panel, work rem sts in St st and *at the same time* work cable inc (see Stitch Guide) on Row 5 and every foll 6th row 21 (23, 21, 23, 24) times—92 (96, 96, 100, 102) sts. Cont even until piece measures 17½" (44.5 cm) or desired length to underarm, ending with Row 4 of chart.

SHAPE CAP |

Row 1: P1, k4, sl next 2 sts onto cn and hold in front of left-hand needle, [k2tog (1 st from each needle)] 2 times, sl 7 sts from right-hand needle to holder, knit to last 9 sts, sl next 2 sts onto cn and hold behind left-hand needle, [k2tog (1 st from each needle)] 2 times, k4, p1—81 (85, 85, 89, 91) sts rem.

Row 2: K1, p6, sl 7 sts from right-hand needle to holder; purl to end of row—74 (78, 78, 82, 84) sts rem.

Dec 1 st each end of needle on next and every foll 6 (4, 4, 6, 6) RS rows, then every other RS row 5 (7, 7, 7, 7) times, then every row 13 times—24 (28, 28, 28, 30) sts rem. BO 5 (5, 5, 5, 6) sts at beg of next 2 rows—14 (18, 18, 18, 18) sts rem. BO all sts.

Finishing

Block pieces to measurements. With yarn threaded on a tapestry needle, sew fronts to back at shoulders.

HOOD | Beg at right front edge, place 14 (17, 17, 18, 18) held sts onto needle. Join yarn and work selvedge and cable pattern over these sts, then pick up and knit 27 sts along front edge, 34 (38, 42, 46, 46) sts along back neck, and 27 sts along left front neck, place other 14 (17, 17, 18, 18) held back sts on needle and work in cable pattern and selvedge—116 (126, 130, 136, 136) sts total. Cont even as established until piece measures 13" (33 cm) from pick-up row, ending with Row 4 of cable panel. **Next row:** Sl 1, k4, sl next 2 sts onto cn and hold in front of left-hand needle, [k2tog (1 st from each needle)] 2 times, knit to last 9 sts, sl next 2 sts onto cn and hold behind left-hand needle, [k2tog (1 st from each needle)] 2 times, k4, sl 1—112 (122, 126, 132, 132) sts rem. Sl 56 (61, 63, 66, 66) sts to spare cir needle, fold hood in half with RS facing tog, and use the three-needle method (see Glossary) to BO the sts tog.

Sew side seams and underarm seams. Sew sleeve caps into armholes, working a three-needle BO to join held underarm sts tog. Sew zipper to center front (see Glossary). Weave in loose ends. Block again lightly.

Lace | Stole

LAURA GRUTZECK

The body of this stole is worked in an interesting lace pattern that looks the same on both sides, and the edging is worked in garter stitch so there's no chance of the "wrong" side showing when you drape it around your shoulders. The stole begins with the zigzag lower edging, then stitches are picked up along the straight side and the body and side edgings are worked for the desired length, then the top edging is worked across the live stitches, binding them off along the way.

Finished Size About 25" (63.5 cm) wide and 75" (190.5 cm) long, blocked.

Yarn Laceweight (#0 Lace).
Shown here: Black Bunny Fibers Laceweight (100% merino wool; 2,400 yd [2,195 m]/8 oz): custom dyed, each skein is unique.

Needles U.S. size 6 (4 mm). Adjust needle size if necessary to obtain the correct gauge.

Notions Markers (m); tapestry needle.

Gauge 26 stitches and 48 rows = 4" (10 cm) in garter stitch, unblocked.

Note

◎ This wrap begins with the edging along the bottom, then stitches are picked up and knitted from the straight edge and the side edgings are worked along with the body. It is finished with the top edging, which is used to bind off all of the stitches.

◎ After the bottom edging is complete, there is no right or wrong side to this shawl—the Porcupine Stitch chart is worked over an odd number of rows and is reversible.

Bottom Edging

CO 8 sts. Work the first point following Rows 1–10 of Bottom Edging chart. Work the second point following Rows 11–20 of the same chart. Rep the last 10 rows 29 more times, ending with Row 20—31 points total. Work the last point following Rows 21–30 of chart. Do not cut yarn.

Body

Turn edging piece sideways and working right to left, pick up and purl (see Glossary) 160 sts along the straight edge of piece just worked, picking up 1 st for every 2 rows of edging, and *at the same time* place marker (pm) after the first 8 sts and before the last 8 sts to denote the side edging sts. Work the first 8 and last 8 sts according to Side Edging chart and center 144 sts according to Porcupine chart as foll:

Row 1: K8 for side edging, work Row 1 of Porcupine chart across 144 sts, then work Row 1 of Side Edging chart across rem 8 sts.

Row 2: Work Row 2 of Side Edging chart across 8 sts, work Row 2 of Porcupine chart across 144 sts, work Row 1 of Side Edging chart across rem 8 sts. Cont in this manner, noting that one side of the edging is always one row behind the other, until Rows 1–9 of Porcupine chart have been worked a total of 59 times—531 rows total.

BOTTOM EDGING

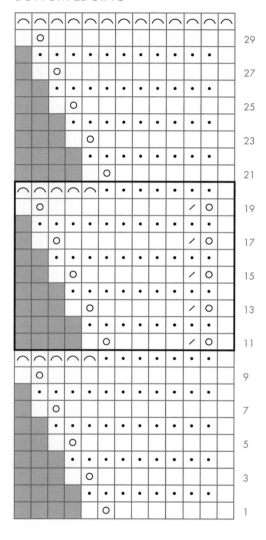

SIDE EDGING

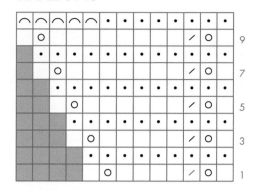

PORCUPINE STITCH

•	p on odd rows; k on even rows	⌒	bind off 1 st
(blank)	k on odd rows; p on even rows	(grey)	no stitch
╱	k2tog	Λ	sl1, k2tog, psso
O	yo	⋇	p3tog
╲	ssk	(bold box)	pattern repeat

TOP EDGING

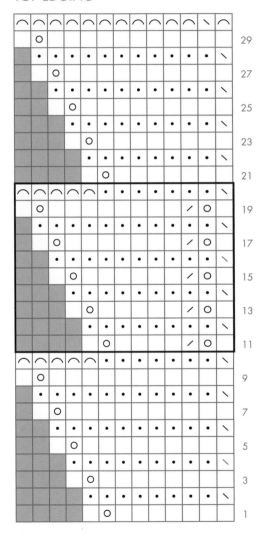

		p on odd rows; k on even rows
		k on odd rows; p on even rows
/		k2tog
O		yo
\		ssk
⌒		bind off 1 st
▨		no stitch
☐		pattern repeat

Top Edging

Use the knitted method (see Glossary) to CO 8 sts onto the tip of the left needle. Work the first point of the top edging onto the body sts following Rows 1–10 of Top Edging chart, working the last st of the edging tog with the first st of the body. Work the second point following Rows 11–20 of the same chart. Rep the last 10 rows 29 more times, ending with Row 20 of chart—31 points total. Work the last point following Rows 21–30 of chart.

Finishing

Wet-block piece to measurements, being careful to maintain distinct points. Weave in loose ends.

Reading Charts

Make your knitting look like the chart: That's the whole story.

Each square on the chart represents a stitch. The square may be a color to represent a yarn color; or it may have a symbol in it to represent either a color or a type of stitch (knit, purl, decrease, etc.). In either case, there should be a key somewhere nearby to translate for you.

Start at the bottom of the chart. Some people like to mark their place with a sticky note under the row they're working; others put the marker above, so they can see how the new row fits over the previous one.

The chart represents the "right," or public, side of the knitted fabric. So if you're looking at the right side of your work, the first stitch you'll knit will be the stitch at the right-hand edge of the chart. If you're looking at the wrong side of your work, your first stitch is the one at the left-hand edge. Most charts have a signal to remind you of this: If the knitting is worked back and forth (flat, so you work a right-side row and then a wrong-side row), the row numbers for the odd-numbered rows will be at the right edge of the chart, and those for the even-numbered rows will be at the left edge; you'll read the chart back and forth in a Z-shaped path. If the knitting is worked in the round, all the round numbers will be at the right edge of the chart—because every time you begin another round, you're at that same spot, beginning with that same stitch.

Fingerless Elbow Gloves

LISA R. MYERS

There are times when we all want to show off a little—do it in style with these extraordinary long and luscious fingerless gloves. Worked at a tight gauge with an assortment of tiny cable patterns (none of which is complicated), these gloves require time and close attention. But don't you think you're worth it? We do!

Finished Size About 8 (8½)" (20.5 [21.5] cm) circumference at upper arm (will stretch to fit larger circumferences), 6 (6½)" (15 [16.5] cm) circumference at wrist, and 21" (53.5 cm) long.

Yarn Sportweight (#2 Fine).
Shown here: Brown Sheep NatureSpun Sport (100% wool, 184 yd [168 m]/50 g): #N64 Platte River Blue, 3 balls.

Needles U.S. size 3 (4) (3.25 [3.5] mm): set of 4 or 5 double-pointed (dpn). Adjust needle size if necessary to obtain the correct gauge.

Notions Cable needle (cn); markers (m); stitch holder or waste yarn; tapestry needle.

Gauge 32 (30) stitches and 34 (32) rows = 4" (10 cm) in stockinette stitch worked in the round; one repeat of Chart 4 = 1¼" (3.2 cm).

Stitch Guide

Twisted Rib (multiple of 2 sts)
Rnd 1: *K1 through back loop (tbl), p1; rep from * to end of rnd.
Repeat this round for pattern.

Notes

◎ These gloves are sized by using different needle sizes. Use the smaller needles for smaller gloves; use the larger needles for larger gloves. The stitch counts are the same for both sizes.

◎ It's important to use a firm tension, both to show the patterning to best effect and to give the gloves a snug fit. Knit a gauge swatch in several of the pattern stitches to check for elasticity: The swatch should stretch but spring back into place.

◎ Don't be tempted to work the traveling stitches without a cable needle. For this project, you'll get better stitch definition if you use a cable needle.

◎ The stitch patterns are surprisingly easy to learn. In general, whenever a knit and purl stitch cross, the knit stitch always travels in front. Whenever two knit stitches cross, the left one travels in front of the right, except for Round 3 of Chart 4, where the second pair is reversed.

Left Glove

CO 66 sts. Place marker (pm) and join for working in rnds, being careful not to twist sts.

ARM | Work in twisted rib (see Stitch Guide) for 7 rnds. **Set-up rnd:** K1 through back loop (tbl), p1, pm, k1tbl, p3, k1tbl, pm, p1, k1tbl, p1, pm, p1, k2tbl, p2, k2tbl, p1, pm, p2tog, k1tbl, M1 pwise (see Glossary), pm, p8, k2tbl, p8, pm, p1, k1tbl, p1, pm, p2tog, k1tbl, M1 pwise, p2, k2tbl, p3, k1tbl, p1, pm, p2tog, k1tbl, M1 pwise, pm, p1, k2tbl, p2, k2tbl, p1, pm, p1—still 66 sts. **Next rnd:** K1tbl, p1, work Rnd 1 of Chart 1 over next 5 sts, p1, k1tbl, p1, work Rnd 1 of Chart 2 over next 8 sts, p1, k1tbl, p1, work Rnd 1 of Chart 3 over next 18 sts, p1, k1tbl, p1, work Rnd 1 of Chart 4 over next 12 sts, p1, k1b, p1, work Rnd 1 of Chart 5 over next 8 sts, p1. Cont in patt as established through Rnd 116 of Chart 3 (note that Chart 3 is broken in three parts), then rep Rnds 113–116 as desired for extra length.

THUMB GUSSET | Work Rnds 117–144 of Chart 3 for thumb gusset and cont in patt as established to end of rnd. **Next rnd:** (Rnd 145) Work in patt to beg of Chart 3, slip 16 thumb sts onto holder, use the backward-loop method (see Glossary) to CO 8 sts over gap, work to end of rnd—58 sts rem.

HAND | Cont in patt as established, working the 8 newly CO sts according to the marked 8 sts of Rows 1–11 of Thumb chart (ignore the other sts on the chart for now) until hand measures desired length. Work 4 rnds in twisted rib. BO all sts in patt.

THUMB | Place 16 held thumb sts onto 2 dpn. With a third dpn, pick up and knit 8 sts along CO sts, then work last 16 sts from Rnd 1 of Thumb chart—66 sts. Work Rnds 2–11 of chart, working marked 8 sts above picked up sts and remaining sts as est. Work 4 rnds in twisted rib. BO all sts in patt.

CHART 1

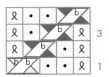

CHART 2

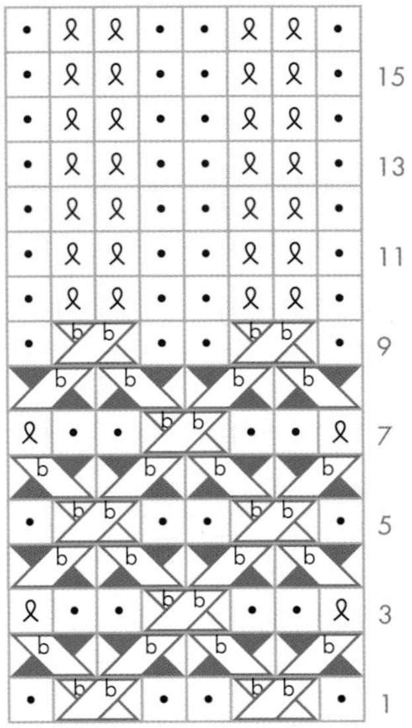

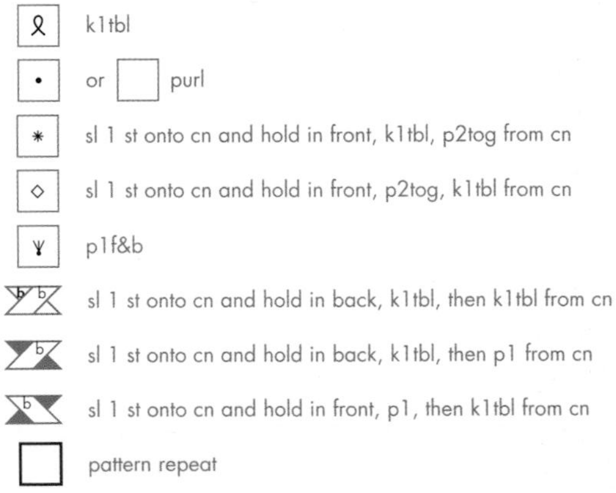

	k1tbl
·	or ☐ purl
✲	sl 1 st onto cn and hold in front, k1tbl, p2tog from cn
◇	sl 1 st onto cn and hold in front, p2tog, k1tbl from cn
⅄	p1f&b
	sl 1 st onto cn and hold in back, k1tbl, then k1tbl from cn
	sl 1 st onto cn and hold in back, k1tbl, then p1 from cn
	sl 1 st onto cn and hold in front, p1, then k1tbl from cn
☐	pattern repeat

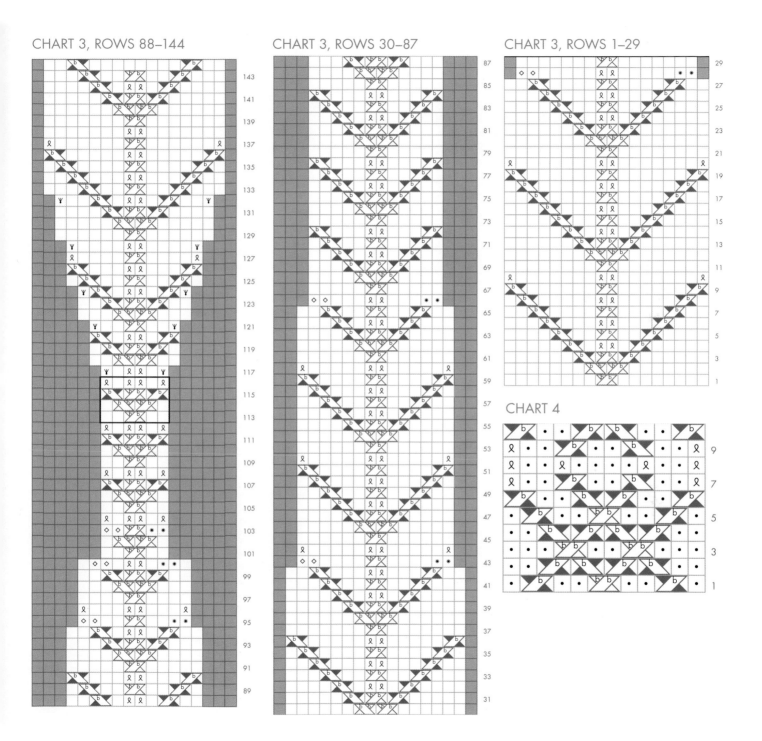

CHART 3, ROWS 88–144

CHART 3, ROWS 30–87

CHART 3, ROWS 1–29

CHART 4

Right Glove

CO 66 sts. Pm and join for working in rnds, being careful not to twist sts. Work in Twisted rib for 7 rnds as for left glove.

Set-up rnd: K1tbl, p1, pm, p1, k2tbl, p2, k2tbl, p2tog, pm, p1, k1tbl, M1 pwise, pm, p1, k1tbl, p3, k2tbl, p2tog, p2, k1tbl, M1 pwise, pm, p1, k1tbl, p1, p8, k2tbl, p8, pm, p2tog, k1tbl, p1, pm, M1 pwise, k2tbl, p2, k2tbl, p1, pm, p1, k1tbl, p1, pm, k1tbl, p3, k1tbl, pm, p1. **Next rnd:** K1tbl, p1, work Rnd 1 of Chart 5 over 8 sts, p1, k1tbl, p1, work Rnd 1 of Chart 4 over 12 sts, p1, k1tbl, p1, work Rnd 1 of Chart 3 over 18 sts, p1, k1tbl, p1, work Rnd 1 of Chart 2 over 8 sts, p1, k1b, p1, work Rnd 1 of Chart 1 over 5 sts, p1. Cont as for left glove.

Finishing

Weave in loose ends. Block lightly.

CHART 5   THUMB CHART

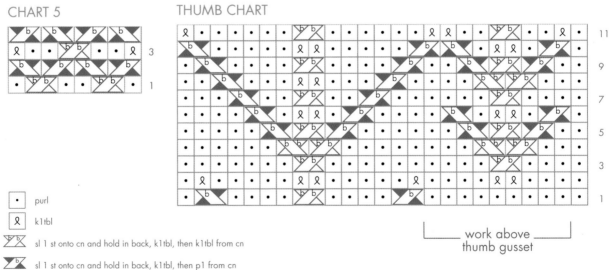

work above
thumb gusset

| · | purl |
| ℓ | k1tbl |

sl 1 st onto cn and hold in back, k1tbl, then k1tbl from cn

sl 1 st onto cn and hold in back, k1tbl, then p1 from cn

sl 1 st onto cn and hold in front, p1, then k1tbl from cn

Abbreviations

beg	begin(s); beginning
BO	bind off
CC	contrast color
cm	centimeter(s)
cn	cable needle
CO	cast on
cont	continue(s); continuing
dec(s)	decrease(s); decreasing
dpn	double-pointed needles
foll	follow(s); following
g	gram(s)
inc(s)	increase(s); increasing
k	knit
k1f&b	knit into the front and back of same stitch
kwise	knitwise, as if to knit
m	marker(s)
MC	main color
mm	millimeter(s)
M1	make one (increase)
M1L	make one left-slant
M1R	make one right-slant
p	purl
p1f&b	purl into the front and back of same stitch
patt(s)	pattern(s)
psso	pass slipped stitch over
pwise	purlwise, as if to purl
rem	remain(s); remaining
rep	repeat(s); repeating
rev St st	reverse stockinette stitch
rnd(s)	round(s)
RS	right side
sl	slip
sl st	slip st (slip 1 stitch purlwise unless otherwise indicated)
ssk	slip 2 stitches knitwise, one at a time, from the left needle to right needle, insert left needle tip through both front loops and knit together from this position (1 stitch decrease)
st	stitch(es)
St st	stockinette stitch
tbl	through back loop
tog	together
WS	wrong side
wyb	with yarn in back
wyf	with yarn in front
yd	yard(s)
yo	yarnover
*	repeat starting point
**	repeat all instructions between asterisks
( )	alternate measurements and/or instructions
[ ]	work instructions as a group a specified number of times

Bind-Offs

THREE-NEEDLE BIND-OFF

Place the stitches to be joined onto two separate needles and hold the needles parallel so that the right sides of knitting face together. Insert a third needle into the first stitch on each of two needles **(Figure 1)** and knit them together as one stitch **(Figure 2)**, *knit the next stitch on each needle the same way, then use the left needle tip to lift the first stitch over the second and off the needle **(Figure 3)**. Repeat from * until no stitches remain on first two needles. Cut yarn and pull tail through last stitch to secure.

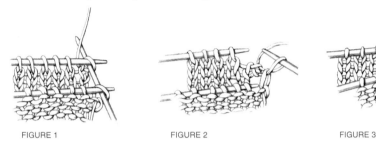

FIGURE 1   FIGURE 2   FIGURE 3

Cast-Ons

BACKWARD-LOOP CAST-ON

*Loop working yarn and place it on needle backward so that it doesn't unwind. Repeat from *.

CABLE CAST-ON

If there are no stitches on the needles, make a slipknot and place it on the left needle, then use the knitted method to cast-on one more stitch (two stitches on needle). Hold needle with working yarn in your left hand with the wrong side of the work facing you. *Insert right needle *between* the first two stitches on left needle **(Figure 1)**, wrap yarn around needle as if to knit, draw yarn through **(Figure 2)**, and place new loop on left needle **(Figure 3)** to form a new stitch. Repeat from * for the desired number of stitches, always working between the first two stitches on the left needle.

FIGURE 1   FIGURE 2   FIGURE 3

KNITTED CAST-ON

Make a slipknot of working yarn and place it on the left needle if there are no stitches already there. *Use the right needle to knit the first stitch (or slipknot) on left needle **(Figure 1)** and place new loop onto left needle to form a new stitch **(Figure 2)**. Repeat from * for the desired number of stitches, always working into the last stitch made.

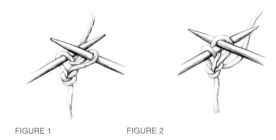

FIGURE 1   FIGURE 2

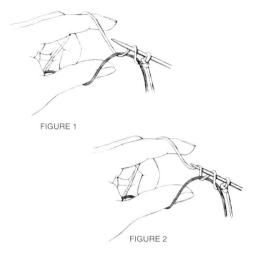

FIGURE 1

FIGURE 2

PROVISIONAL INVISIBLE CAST-ON

Make a loose slipknot of working yarn and place it on the right needle. Hold a length of contrasting waste yarn next to the slipknot and around your left thumb; hold working yarn over your left index finger. *Bring the right needle forward under waste yarn, over working yarn, grab a loop of working yarn **(Figure 1)**, then bring needle back behind the working yarn and grab a second loop **(Figure 2)**. Repeat from * for the desired number of stitches. When you're ready to work in the opposite direction, place the exposed loops on a knitting needle as you pull out the waste yarn.

Decreases

KNIT 2 TOGETHER (K2TOG)

Knit two stitches together as if they were a single stitch.

PURL 2 TOGETHER (P2TOG)

Purl two stitches together as if they were a single stitch.

PURL 2 TOGETHER THROUGH BACK LOOPS (P2TOGTBL)

Bring right needle tip behind two stitches on left needle, enter through the back loop of the second stitch, then the first stitch, then purl them together.

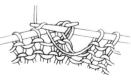

SLIP, SLIP, KNIT (SSK)

Slip two stitches individually knitwise **(Figure 1)**, insert left needle tip into the front of these two slipped stitches, and use the right needle to knit them together through their back loops **(Figure 2)**.

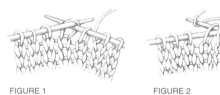

FIGURE 1   FIGURE 2

SLIP, SLIP, SLIP, KNIT (SSSK)

Slip three stitches individually knitwise **(Figure 1)**, insert left needle tip into the front of these three slipped stitches, and use the right needle to knit them together through their back loops **(Figure 2)**.

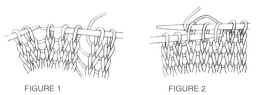

FIGURE 1   FIGURE 2

I-Cord (also called Knit-Cord)

Using two double-pointed needles, cast on the desired number of stitches (usually three to four). *Without turning the needle, slide stitches to other end of needle, pull the yarn around the back, and knit the stitches as usual. Repeat from * for desired length.

Increases

RAISED MAKE-ONE—LEFT SLANT (M1L)

Note: Use the left slant if no direction of slant is specified. With left needle tip, lift the strand between the last knitted stitch and the first stitch on the left needle from front to back **(Figure 1)**, then knit the lifted loop through the back **(Figure 2)**.

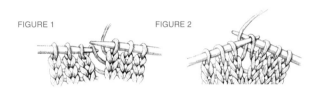

FIGURE 1   FIGURE 2

RAISED MAKE-ONE—RIGHT SLANT (M1R)

With left needle tip, lift the strand between the needles from back to front **(Figure 1)**. Knit the lifted loop through the front **(Figure 2)**.

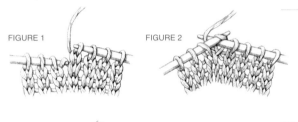

FIGURE 1   FIGURE 2

RAISED MAKE-ONE PURLWISE (M1 PWISE)

With left needle tip, lift the strand between the needles from back to front **(Figure 1)**, then purl the lifted loop through the front **(Figure 2)**.

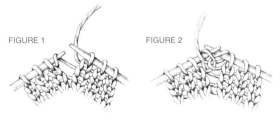

FIGURE 1   FIGURE 2

Pick Up and Purl

With purl side of work facing and working from right to left, *insert needle tip under selvedge stitch from the far side to the near side, wrap yarn around needle purlwise **(Figure 1)**, and pull a loop through **(Figure 2)**. Repeat from * for desired number of stitches.

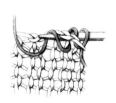

FIGURE 1   FIGURE 2

Seams
KITCHENER STITCH

Arrange stitches on two needles so that there is the same number of stitches on each needle. Hold the needles parallel to each other with wrong sides of the knitting together. Allowing about ½" (1.3 cm) per stitch to be grafted, thread matching yarn on a tapestry needle. Work from right to left as follows:

Step 1. Bring tapestry needle through the first stitch on the front needle as if to purl and leave the stitch on the needle.

Step 2. Bring tapestry needle through the first stitch on the back needle as if to knit and leave that stitch on the needle.

Step 3. Bring tapestry needle through the first front stitch as if to knit and slip this stitch off the needle, then bring tapestry needle through the next front stitch as if to purl and leave this stitch on the needle.

Step 4. Bring tapestry needle through the first back stitch as if to purl and slip this stitch off the needle, then bring tapestry needle through the next back stitch as if to knit and leave this stitch on the needle.

Repeat Steps 3 and 4 until one stitch remains on each needle, adjusting the tension to match the rest of the knitting as you go. To finish, bring tapestry needle through the front stitch as if to knit and slip this stitch off the needle, then bring tapestry needle through the back stitch as if to purl and slip this stitch off the needle.

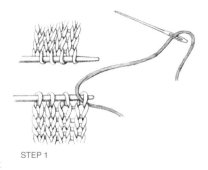

STEP 1

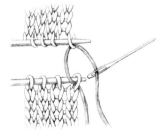

STEP 2

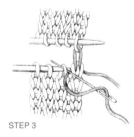

STEP 3

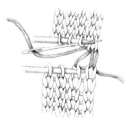

STEP 4

MATTRESS STITCH

Insert threaded needle under one bar between the two edge stitches on one piece **(Figure 1)**, then under the corresponding bar plus the bar above it on the other piece **(Figure 2).** *Pick up the next two bars on the first piece **(Figure 3)**, then the next two bars on the other. Repeat from *, ending by picking up the last bar or pair of bars on the first piece. To reduce bulk in the mattress stitch seam, work as for the one-stitch seam allowance but pick up the bars in the center of the edge stitches instead of between the last two stitches.

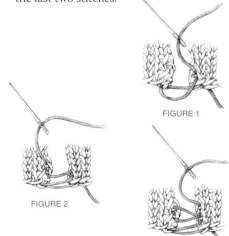

FIGURE 1

FIGURE 2

FIGURE 3

Short-Rows

KNIT SIDE

Work to turning point, slip next stitch purlwise (**Figure 1**), bring the yarn to the front, then slip the same stitch back to the left needle (**Figure 2**), turn the work around and bring the yarn in position for the next stitch—one stitch has been wrapped and the yarn is correctly positioned to work the next stitch. When you come to a wrapped stitch on a subsequent row, hide the wrap by working it together with the wrapped stitch as follows: Insert right needle tip under the wrap from the front (**Figure 3**) then into the stitch on the needle, and work the stitch and its wrap together as a single stitch.

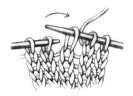

FIGURE 1

FIGURE 2

FIGURE 3

PURL SIDE

Work to the turning point, slip the next stitch purlwise to the right needle, bring the yarn to the back of the work (**Figure 1**), return the slipped stitch to the left needle, bring the yarn to the front between the needles (**Figure 2**), and turn the work so that the knit side is facing—one stitch has been wrapped and the yarn is correctly positioned to knit the next stitch. To hide the wrap on a subsequent purl row, work to the wrapped stitch, use the tip of the right needle to pick up the wrap from the back, place it on the left needle (**Figure 3**), then purl it together with the wrapped stitch.

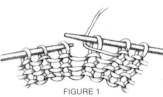

FIGURE 1

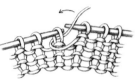

FIGURE 2

FIGURE 3

Zipper

With right side facing and zipper closed, pin zipper to the knitted pieces so edges cover the zipper teeth. With contrasting thread and right side facing, baste zipper in place close to teeth (**Figure 1**). Turn work over and with matching sewing thread and needle, stitch outer edges of zipper to wrong side of knitting (**Figure 2**), being careful to follow a single column of stitches in the knitting to keep zipper straight. Turn work back to right side facing, and with matching sewing thread, sew knitted fabric close to teeth (**Figure 3**). Remove basting.

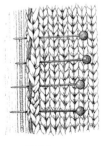

FIGURE 1

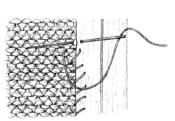

FIGURE 2

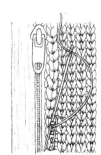

FIGURE 3

Black Bunny Fibers
http://blackbunnyfibers.etsy.com
   Laceweight

Blackberry Ridge
Woolen Mill
3776 Forshaug Rd.
Mt. Horeb, WI 53572
www.blackberry-ridge.com
   Cotton Blend

Brown Sheep Company
100662 County Rd. 16
Mitchell, NE 69357
www.brownsheep.com
   NatureSpun Sport

Classic Elite Yarns
122 Western Ave.
Lowell, MA 01851
www.classiceliteyarns.com
   Wool Bamboo

Dale of Norway
4750 Shelburne Rd.
Shelburne, VT 05482
www.dale.no
   Svale
   Stork

Garnstudio
www.garnstudio.com
   Drops Alpaca

JaggerSpun
Box 188
Springvale, ME 04083
www.jaggerspun.com
   Zephyr

Koigu Wool Designs
Box 158
Chatsworth, ON, Canada N0H1G0
www.koigu.com
   Painter's Palette Merino
   Koigu Premium Merino

Skacel Collection Inc./Zitron
Box 88110
Seattle, WA 98138
www.skacelknitting.com
   Zitron Trekking XXL
   Zitron Kokon

Tahki Stacy Charles Inc./
Filatura di Crosa
70-30 80th St. Bldg. 36
Ridgewood, NY 11385
www.tahkistacycharles.com
   Filatura di Crosa Zarina

Unique Kolours/Colinette
28 N. Bacton Hill Rd.
Malvern, PA 19355
www.uniquekolours.com
   Colinette Tao

Westminster Fibers/Jaeger/
Regia/Rowan
165 Ledge St.
Nashua, NH 03060
www.westminsterfibers.com
   Regia Silk
   Rowan 4-Ply Soft
   Rowan Cashcotton 4-ply
   Rowan Cashsoft 4-Ply
   Rowan Classic Yarn Bamboo Soft
   Rowan Kid Silk Haze

Fit and Garment Construction

Budd, Ann. *The Knitter's Handy Book of Sweater Patterns.* Loveland, Colorado: Interweave Press, 2004.
Includes a blueprint for creating sweaters, as well as extensive information on fit, shoulder styles, and other ways to individualize garments to the wearer's measurements.

Moreno, Jillian, and Amy R. Singer. *Big Girl Knits.* New York: Potter Craft, 2006.
Excellent discussion of sweater design as it relates to plus-size fit.

Newton, Deborah. *Designing Knitwear.* Newtown, Connecticut: Taunton Press, 1998.
An incredible amount of information on designing patterns for handknits.

Righetti, Maggie. *Sweater Design in Plain English.* New York: St. Martin's/Griffin, 1990.
Comprehensive overview of sweater design and fit.

Walker, Barbara G. *Knitting from the Top.* Pittsville, Wisconsin: Schoolhouse Press, 1996.
Learn how to design and knit any type of garment in one piece, from the top down.

Zimmermann, Elizabeth. *Knitting Without Tears.* New York: Fireside/Simon & Schuster, 1995.
Humorous yet information-packed volume on knitting in general, including issues relating to garment structure and fit.

Vintage Styles Updated for Today's Knitters

Avery, Véronik. *Knitting Classic Style.* New York: Stewart Tabori & Chang, 2007.
Contemporary-styled garments inspired by fashion's archives.

Bush, Nancy. *Knitting Vintage Socks.* Loveland, Colorado: Interweave Press, 2005.
Packed with lovely sock patterns inspired by vintage publications.

Dallas, Sarah, with Yesterknits. *Vintage Knits: 30 Exquisite Vintage-Inspired Patterns for Cardigans, Twin Sets, Crewnecks and More.* New York: Simon & Schuster, 2002.
Knitting patterns based on original vintage patterns from the Yesterknits collection.

Hargreaves, Kim, et al. *Vintage Knits: Thirty Knitting Designs for Men and Women.* North Pomfret, Vermont: Trafalgar Square, 2005.
Loosely based on fashion from the 1940s through 1960s, drawing from old films, vintage photographs, and pattern archives.

Sowerby, Jane. *Victorian Lace Today.* Sioux Falls, South Dakota: XRX Books, 2006.
Lovely lace garments and shawls based on Victorian-era patterns and stitches.

Waller, Jane. *Knitting Fashions of the 1940s.* Ramsbury: Crowood Press, 2006.
Fascinating combination of social history as it meets knitting, featuring many vintage photographs side by side with the updated garments.

Ethnic and Traditional Styles

Bush, Nancy. *Folk Socks.* Loveland, Colorado: Interweave Press, 1994.
Excellent overview of folk-sock-knitting traditions from around the world.

Druchunas, Donna. *Arctic Lace.* Fort Collins, Colorado: Nomad Press, 2006.
History of lace knitting among the Native American peoples of Alaska, with patterns and photographs.

Finseth, Margarethe. *Norsk Strikkedesign.* Petaluma, California: Unicorn Books, 2002.
Collection of sweaters based on Norwegian folk knitting and folk costume.

Gibson-Roberts, Priscilla. *Ethnic Socks & Stockings.* Sioux Falls, South Dakota: XRX Books, 1995.
In-depth information on Turkish and other Eastern European socks and stockings noted for exquisite color work.

–––. *Knitting in the Old Way.* Fort Collins, Colorado: Nomad Press, 2005.
Review of folk sweater styles from around the world.

Keele, Wendy. *Poems of Color.* Loveland, Colorado: Interweave Press, 1995.
History of Swedish Bohus knitting, along with updated patterns from the Bohus archives.

McGregor, Sheila. *Traditional Fair Isle Knitting.* Mineola, New York: Dover, 2003.
Charts and other technical information on stranded knitting from the northern islands of Britain.

Oberle, Cheryl. *Folk Shawls.* Loveland, Colorado: Interweave Press, 2000.
Collection of shawls inspired by worldwide traditions.

backward-loop cast-on 136
Big Girl Knits 13
bind-off, three-needle 136
blocking 29
blocking wires 29

cable cast-on 136
caps 15
cast-ons 136–137
color work 16
costs, yarn 18–19

decreases 137
decreases, marking stitch 27
drape, yarn 22
durability, yarn 19

ease, garment 12
ethnic handknitting 17

Fair Isle color 16
fiber content 22–23
finishing 29
fit, garment 11–14

gauge 12, 15, 23, 30
gauge, needle size, and yarn chart 7

I-cord 138
increases 138
increases, marking stitch 27
intarsia color 16

Kitchener stitch 139
knit-cord see I-cord
knit 2 together (k2tog) 137
knitted cast-on 136
Knitting Without Tears 18

lace shawl 14
lifeline 28–29
lighting 28

markers, stitch 26–27
marking stitches 26–27
mattress stitch 139
measurements, garment 11– 12
Moreno, Jillian 13

needles 24–26
needle size, yarn, and gauge chart 7

pattern repeats 15; marking 27
pick up and purl 138
point protectors 28
provisional invisible cast-on 136
purl 2 together (p2tog) 137
purl 2 together through back loops
    (p2togtbl) 137

raised make-one—left slant (M1L) 138
raised make-one—purlwise (M1 pwise) 138
raised make-one—right slant (M1R) 138

schematics 11
seams 12, 139
short-rows 140
Singer, Amy 13
slip, slip, knit (ssk) 137
slip, slip, slip, knit (sssk) 137
socks 15
stitch markers 26–27
stitch pattern length 16
stitch patterns, marking 27
substitution, yarn 22
swatching, gauge 23, 30; practice 28

tangles, avoiding yarn 23–24
three-needle bind-off 136
twin set 14–15

Walker, Barbara 15
Walker, Jane 17
wearability, garment 14

vintage style 16–17
yarn, center-pull ball 23–24;
    needle size and gauge chart 7
yarn costs 18–19
yarn drape 22
yarn durability 19
yarn selection 21–23
yarn substitution 22
yarn tangles, avoiding 23–24

Zimmermann, Elizabeth 18
zippers 140